XML In, Web Out: International Symposium on sub rosa XML

AA006174

Balisage Series on Markup Technologies Volume 18

Washington, DC, USA
1 August 2016

ISBN: 978-1-5108-3880-2

Printed from e-media with permission by:

Curran Associates, Inc.
57 Morehouse Lane
Red Hook, NY 12571

Some format issues inherent in the e-media version may also appear in this print version.

Copyright© (2016) by Mulberry Technologies, Inc.
All rights reserved.

Printed by Curran Associates, Inc. (2017)

For permission requests, please contact Mulberry Technologies, Inc.
at the address below.

Mulberry Technologies, Inc.
17 West Jefferson Street, Suite 207
Rockville, MD 20850
USA

Phone: 301/315-9631
Fax: 301/315-8285

info@mulberrytech.com

Additional copies of this publication are available from:

Curran Associates, Inc.
57 Morehouse Lane
Red Hook, NY 12571 USA
Phone: 845-758-0400
Fax: 845-758-2633
Email: curran@proceedings.com
Web: www.proceedings.com

Table of Contents

Balisage Series on Markup Technologies

Vol 18. Proceedings of XML In, Web Out: International Symposium on sub rosa XML

XML In, Web Out: International Symposium on sub rosa XML

Washington, DC

August 1, 2016

Page:

1 Brüggemann-Klein, Anne. "The XML Expert's Path to Web Applications: Lessons learned from document and from software engineering." Presented at XML In, Web Out: International Symposium on sub rosa XML, Washington, DC, August 1, 2016. In *Proceedings of XML In, Web Out: International Symposium on sub rosa XML*. Balisage Series on Markup Technologies, vol. 18 (2016). DOI: 10.4242/BalisageVol18.Bruggemann-Klein01.

7 Caton, Paul, and Miguel Vieira. "The Kiln XML Publishing Framework." Presented at XML In, Web Out: International Symposium on sub rosa XML, Washington, DC, August 1, 2016. In *Proceedings of XML In, Web Out: International Symposium on sub rosa XML*. Balisage Series on Markup Technologies, vol. 18 (2016). DOI: 10.4242/BalisageVol18.Caton01.

17 Clark, Ashley M., and Sarah Connell. "Meta(data)morphosis." Presented at XML In, Web Out: International Symposium on sub rosa XML, Washington, DC, August 1, 2016. In *Proceedings of XML In, Web Out: International Symposium on sub rosa XML*. Balisage Series on Markup Technologies, vol. 18 (2016). DOI: 10.4242/BalisageVol18.Clark01.

43 Feldman, Damon. "Message Format Persistence in Large Enterprise Systems." Presented at XML In, Web Out: International Symposium on sub rosa XML, Washington, DC, August 1, 2016. In *Proceedings of XML In, Web Out: International Symposium on sub rosa XML*. Balisage Series on Markup Technologies, vol. 18 (2016). DOI: 10.4242/BalisageVol18.Feldman01.

63 Kraetke, Martin, and Gerrit Imsieke. "XSLT as a Modern, Powerful Static Website Generator: Publishing Hogrefe's Clinical Handbook of Psychotropic Drugs as a Web

App." Presented at XML In, Web Out: International Symposium on sub rosa XML, Washington, DC, August 1, 2016. In *Proceedings of XML In, Web Out: International Symposium on sub rosa XML*. Balisage Series on Markup Technologies, vol. 18 (2016). DOI: 10.4242/BalisageVol18.Kraetke02.

74 Murray, Gregory. "XQuery is not (just) a query language: Web application development with XQuery." Presented at XML In, Web Out: International Symposium on sub rosa XML, Washington, DC, August 1, 2016. In *Proceedings of XML In, Web Out: International Symposium on sub rosa XML*. Balisage Series on Markup Technologies, vol. 18 (2016). DOI: 10.4242/BalisageVol18.Murray01.

There is nothing so practical as a good theory

Link to the Balisage Proceedings Home Page at http://www.balisage.net/Proceedings
Link to this paper (entry page with links) at http://www.balisage.net/Proceedings/vol18/html/Bruggemann-Klein01/BalisageVol18-Bruggemann-Klein01.html

XML In, Web Out: International Symposium on sub rosa XML
Proceedings

The XML Expert's Path to Web Applications

Lessons learned from document and from software engineering

Anne Brüggemann-Klein
Technical University of Munich (TUM)
<brueggemann-klein@tum.de>

XML In, Web Out: International Symposium on sub rosa XML
August 1, 2016

Copyright © 2016 by the author. Used with permission.

How to cite this paper

Brüggemann-Klein, Anne. "The XML Expert's Path to Web Applications: Lessons learned from document and from software engineering." Presented at XML In, Web Out: International Symposium on sub rosa XML, Washington, DC, August 1, 2016. In *Proceedings of XML In, Web Out: International Symposium on sub rosa XML*. Balisage Series on Markup Technologies, vol. 18 (2016). DOI: 10.4242/BalisageVol18.Bruggemann-Klein01.

Abstract

Web applications offer a golden opportunity for domain experts who work with XML documents to leverage their domain expertise, their knowledge of document engineering principles, and their skills in XML technology. Current XML technologies provide a full stack of modeling languages, implementation languages, and tools for Web applications that is stable, platform independent, and based on open standards. Combining principles and proven practices from document and software engineering, we identify architectures, modeling techniques, and implementation strategies that let end-user developers who are conversant with XML technologies create their own Web applications.

Table of Contents

Introduction
Domain modeling and implementation of the server component
The server component as an event-driven system
Connececting the server component to Web clients
Multi-client Web applications
Conclusion

Introduction

The core uses of XML technologies in document engineering are to encode structured, mostly text-based information (XML), to impose validity constraints on XML-encoded documents (DTD, XML Schema,

Relax NG), to translate, often for presentation purposes, XML-encoded information into alternative formats (XSLT) and to query a data layer of XML-encoded information (XQuery). Typical applications are information systems for publishing and documentation.

This paper discusses how to repurpose XML technologies for Web applications. It turns out that current XML technologies provide a full stack of modeling and implementation languages and tools for Web applications that is stable, platform independent and based on open standards. Most importantly, it works right on top of HTTP. It is bare-bones in the sense that it requires little to no glue in the form of an application framework. This is a golden opportunity for domain experts who work with XML documents to leverage their domain expertise, their knowledge of document engineering principles and their skills in XML technology to build Web applications. This lets us pluck a handful of low-hanging fruits from the tree of XML technology for Web applications besides familiarity and accessability, such as platform and vendor independence, stability, reliance on open standards and end-to-end XML-based data encoding without costly impedence mismatches. Combining principles and proven practices from document and from software engineering, we examine and propose architectures, modeling techniques and implementation strategies that let end-user developers who are conversant with XML technologies create their own Web applications.

Our claim in this paper is not so much that we have invented something completely new. Rather, we review what is known, tailor it to the general domain of Web applications and package it as a consistent set of practices. We demonstrate our approach with the well-known casino game Blackjack, drawing on previous work, particularly on our browser game case study GameX [SKB14][BSK15].

A word about the state of this paper: The ideas that are presented in this paper have been at the heart of research and teaching in my group at TUM for a number of years. Pertinent aspects are summarized in previous papers at Balisage as cited above, in a recent PhD thesis [S16] and in recent Bachelor [O16] Master [T16] Theses. I intend this paper to connect previous results and to integrate them into a holistic set of practices. I continue to refine and validate these practices using the games Blackjack and Mancala in a lab course on XML technology at TUM that I teach in the current summer term 2016. At this stage of writing, I discuss principles and practices mostly in the abstract. The final version of the paper will draw on a fully worked example, the game Blackjack.

A Web application by definition follows the client-server architecture. In this paper, we consider *thin-client* Web applications. The core of the application runs in a server component that is accessed by client components through a Web server. The client components run in Web browsers; they display relevant information and offer interaction alternatives. A chosen interaction is translated into an HTTP request which is processed by the server component, resulting in an update of the relevant information to display, which is then returned to the client in the form of an HTTP response. This implies that the server component of a Web application is best viewed as an event-driven system which is ultimately triggered by HTTP requests.

In the further four sections of this paper, we address four aspects of XML-powered Web applications: First, we investigate how to implement an object-oriented, domain-driven design for the server component of a Web application with XML technologies, focusing on the principle of encapsulation. Second, we address the event-driven nature of the server component, employing statechart modeling encoded with SCXML. In particular, we define a stratification criterion that ensures that the behaviour that is expressed through the statechart can be executed in the framework of the request-response cycle of a Web application. Third, we put the server component on the Web, following the model-view-controler and XRX architectural styles. Fourth and finally, we discuss requirements and some solutions for multi-client Web applications that need to implement the observer pattern and server push interactions. We conclude with a reflection and with some final remarks.

Domain modeling and implementation of the server component

From a document engineering perspective, the server component of a Web application is typically seen as a repository of documents that is accessed through query and update functions. However, some types of Web applications have state in the server component beyond the state of a typical backend data layer. Specifically, they require several instances of the server component on one Web server that are dynamically instantiated and destroyed under user control. This is not the case with GameX, where all players share a single map to play on, but it is the case with Blackjack, where each table of Blackjack requires its own instance of a Blackjack game to be created in the server component, even in the most simple single-player scenario.

From a software engineering and particularly from an object-oriented perspective, the data of the server component are often naturally organized into a number of interrelated objects, with methods that locally operate on the data of an object, using methods on other objects as services. This is the principle of encapsulation, a form of abstraction that together with information hiding and inheritance facilitates software qualities such as ease of maintenance and extensibility.

More precisely, coming from an object-oriented modeling [BD] and domain-driven perspective [E04], an application is typically modeled in the object-oriented style by a number of classes, with a class corresponding to a type of domain entity and defining which data an instance of the class (that is, an object), holds and which methods can be performed on these data. This approach is particularly appropriate for Web applications that have state as described above.

We demonstrate how to model the data part of a class with a class schema in XML Schema. Objects are then implemented as XML elements that conform to their class schema. Methods are implemented as XQuery functions that have a reference to the object they are operating on as a "self" or "this" parameter. This approach mirrors directly common implementation practice for methods in object oriented programming languages.

The most simple version of our case study Blackjack provides a game server to which eventually, due to this strategy of encapsulation, a number of clients can connect independently and asynchronously to play their own, separate one-person single-round games of Blackjack.

The domain model for Blackjack at this stage comprises the data of a single Blackjack game such as player hand, dealer hand and player bet. In addition, there are a number of top-level activities that operate on these data, such as placing a bet, executing a hit or stand command or tallying the game. There are also activities for creating and destroying a game and some helper activities that are invoked by top-level activities, for example instantiating and shuffling a deck of cards or drawing a card from the deck. The data model is defined by a UML class diagram which is then translated into XML Schema. The activities are implemented in an XQuery module, using the encapsulation technique described earlier.

The server component as an event-driven system

In the previous section, we have not yet addressed the overall behaviour of the server component. We view the server component as an event-driven system whose top-level activities are triggered by events, most commonly by user actions. Typically, there are constraints to the legal sequences of events, and the specific activity that is triggered may be dependent only on a specific pattern in the history of previous events. The classical tool to model the behaviour of an event-driven system is statecharts. Statecharts have been first introduced by Harel as documented in a book [HP98] he co-authored with Politi. They have later, in the object-oriented variant of state diagrams, become part of UML2; see [SSHK15] for a textbook introduction and [H99] for an extensive discussion of the use of statecharts in software engineering. Most recently, with SCXML [B15], an XML encoding language for statecharts has been standardized, bringing statecharts into the realm of XML technologies. A number of research papers discuss use of SCXML in particular, among them the Bachelor Thesis of Roxendal [R10], invited expert to the W3C committee that defined SCXML.

We complement our domain model of Blackjack with a UML statechart diagram that models the behaviour of the server component. The statechart is triggered by events that eventually originate from HTTP requests on behalf of a player who operates a Blackjack client component running in a Web browser. Execution of the statechart may result in computing data that are returned to the client component as a HTTP response. The statechart needs to be stratified in the sense that each execution of the statechart gives rise to an alternating sequence of events triggered by HTTP requests and returns of data in a HTTP response. The returned data specify which potential next actions on the part of the user will be accepted according to the statechart in its current state, following the principles of REST [F00].

The UML statechart diagram is manually translated into an SCXML encoding, following straightforward procedures, so in principle this translation can be automated. The SCXML statechart is then implemented in yet another XQuery module. Following the command pattern, ultimately each event results in a call to a query which operates on XML data representing the current state and on the SCXML data themselves.

Connececting the server component to Web clients

We are now ready to put the server component on the Web. We deploy the server component in an XML database system on the Web, currently we use eXist, but system dependencies are minimal. Browsers who wish to initiate a new Blackjack game connect to a dispatcher XQuery file on the server, which in turn instantiates a new Blackjack server component cum statechart object. From then on, communication between the browser and the server component is mediated by a controler query which translates HTTP requests from the browser into events for its statechart and translates data from the statechart into HTTP responses. The Blackjack client is implemented in XForms. It holds the information it is to display and the interactions it is to enable in its model, submitting requests AJAX-style and receiving responses in its model. The architecture is an instance of the model-view-controler architectural style named model-view-presenter with passive view and passive model [F02] and a one-to-one relationship between presenter and model.

Multi-client Web applications

It is straightforward to extend the Blackjack game to multiple players playing at multiple tables as long as all players at one table play through the same browser. The situation changes completely if we want to support a truly distributed game in which each player at a Blackjack table plays through their own browser. In that case, we have a number of controlers, one per player, who each are able to forward commands from "their" player to the server object and play back any data that the server component returns, possibly in reaction to commands issued by another controler. The latter destroys the ping-pong rhythm of request and response in the HTTP protocol. In this type of communication, which is actually a type of server broadcast, a server needs to be able to push responses to clients from whom there is no open request.

There are ways to emulate the server-push or server-broadcast communication pattern over HTTP by using so-called "busy polling" or "long polling" techniques in combination with AJAX-like requests. In fact, our browser game GameX uses busy polling to propagate changes in the map that were caused by one player to all other players. However, these solutions are not stable and do not scale. HTML5-based architectures go beyond the request-response cycle of the HTTP protocol towards server push solutions by supporting APIs such as Server-Sent Events and WebSockets [WSM13] in the client and with corresponding server-side implementations, for example in Node.js [HW12]. There does not seem to exist an XML-savvy implementation of these approaches, yet.

Conclusion

In this paper, we have laid out a coherent and coordinated set of practices for developing XML-powered Web applications. With Blackjack, this paper provides a worked example that illustrates these practices. The practices draw on previous work and are have been and are being bullet-proofed with further case studies.

One source of inspiration have been proven principles and practices from software engineering. We have demonstrated how the principle of encapsulation can be emulated with XML technology by mapping objects and methods operating on objects to XML elements and XQuery-encoded activities that are parameterized with the object-element they are supposed to operate on as a "self" or "this" parameter.

From data model to a model that also addresses actions: (1) defining a domain model. (2) data-behaviour-activities: modeling state with statemachine diagrams, encoded in SCXML. This facilitates model-driven code generation.

By systematically analysing the model-view-controler (MVC) architectural style and how it can be applied in the context of Web applications and the request-response cycle, we have worked out how a server component can be kept independent of its clients as long as there is a one-to-one relationship between a client and an instance object that the server component creates for the client to interact with.

The challenge is how to design an XML-driven solution for real multi-client applications or, more precisely, how to realize the observer pattern in the XML context. HTML5-based architectures go beyond the request-response cycle of the HTTP protocol towards server push solutions by supporting APIs such as Server-Sent Events and WebSockets in the client and with corresponding server-side implementations, for example in Node.js. If we wish to rely solely on XML technolgies, the only options seem to be emulations of server push through long pulling or busy pulling. It is a point for discussion and further development if we can fill this gap better with technologies in the XML stack.

The practices proposed in this paper are compatible with domain-driven design and model-driven solutions.

References

[B15] Jim Barnett (Editor-in-Chief). “State Chart XML (SCXML): State Machine Notation for Control Abstraction.” W3C Recommendation 1 September 2015. [online]. [cited 11 April 2016]. http://www.w3.org/TR/2015/REC-scxml-20150901/.

[BD] Bernd Brügge; Allen Dutoit. “Object-Oriented Software Engineering Using UML, Patterns, and Java”. Prentice Hall, 2009.

[BSK15] Anne Brüggemann-Klein; Marouane Sayih; Zlatina Keskivov. “Statecharts and State Chart XML as a Modeling Technique in Web Engineering”. In *Proceedings of Balisage: The Markup Conference 2015*. Balisage Series on Markup Technologies, vol. 15 (2015). [online]. [cited 11 April 2016]. http://www.balisage.net/Proceedings/vol15/html/Sayih01/BalisageVol15-Sayih01.html. doi:10.4242/BalisageVol15.Sayih01.

[E04] Eric Evans. “Domain-Driven Design: Tackling Complexity in the Heart of Software”. Addison-Wesley, 2004.

[F00] Roy Thomas Fielding. “Architectural Styles and the Design of Network-based Software Architectures”. PhD Thesis University of California, Irvine 2000.

[F02] Martin Fowler. “Patterns of Enterprise Application Architecture”. Addison-Wesley, 2002.

[F11] Martin Fowler. “Domain-Specific Languages”. Addison-Wesley, 2011.

[H99] Ian Horrocks. “Constructing the User Interface with Statecharts”. Addison-Wesley 1999.

[HP98] David Harel; Michal Politi. “Modeling Reactive Systems with Statecharts: The STATEMATE Approach”. McGraw-Hill, 1998. [online] [cited 19 2016] http://www.wisdom.weizmann.ac.il/~harel /reactive_systems.html.

[HW12] Tom Hughes-Croucher; Mike Wilson. “Node: Up and Running: Scalable Server-Side Code with JavaScript.” O'Reilly 2012.

[R10] Johan Roxendal. “Managing Web Based Dialog Systems Using StateChart XML.” Bachelor Thesis University of Gothenburg 2010.

[S16] Marouane Sayih “Web Engineering mit XML-Technologien”. PhD Thesis, 2016. [submitted at TUM].

[SKB14] Marouane Sayih; Martin Kuhn; Anne Brüggemann-Klein. “GameX — Event-Based Programming with XML Technology”. In *Proceedings of Balisage: The Markup Conference 2014*. Balisage Series on Markup Technologies, vol. 13 (2014). [online]. [cited 20 April 2016]. http://www.balisage.net /Proceedings/vol13/html/Bruggemann-Klein01/BalisageVol13-Bruggemann-Klein01.html. doi:10.4242/BalisageVol13.Bruggemann-Klein01.

[SSHK15] Martina Seidl; Marion Scholz; Christian Huemer; Gerti Kappel. “UML@Classroom. An Introduction to Object-Oriented Modeling”. Springer-Verlag 2015.

[T16] Nina Tanakova. “Domain-Driven Design for Web Applications with XML-Technology”. Master Thesis TUM, 2016.

[O16] Jakob Oelkers. “Modeling and Implementing a Distributed 2-Person Board Game with XML Technology”. Bachelor Thesis TUM, 2016.

[WSM13] Vanessa Wang; Frank Salim; Peter Moskovits. “The Definite Guide to HTML5 WebSocket”. APress 2013.

Author's keywords for this paper: Web Application; XML Technology; Document Engineering; Software Engineering; Architecture; Modeling; Implementation; End-User Programming

Link to the Balisage Proceedings Home Page at http://www.balisage.net/Proceedings
Link to this paper (entry page with links) at http://www.balisage.net/Proceedings/vol18/html/Caton01/BalisageVol18-Caton01.html

XML In, Web Out: International Symposium on sub rosa XML
Proceedings

The Kiln XML Publishing Framework

Paul Caton
Research Analyst, King's Digital Laboratory
King's College, London
<paul.caton@kcl.ac.uk>

Miguel Vieira
Software Engineer, King's Digital Laboratory
King's College, London
<jose.m.vieira@kcl.ac.uk>

XML In, Web Out: International Symposium on sub rosa XML
August 1, 2016

Copyright © 2016 by the authors. Used with permission.

How to cite this paper

Caton, Paul, and Miguel Vieira. "The Kiln XML Publishing Framework." Presented at XML In, Web Out: International Symposium on sub rosa XML, Washington, DC, August 1, 2016. In *Proceedings of XML In, Web Out: International Symposium on sub rosa XML*. Balisage Series on Markup Technologies, vol. 18 (2016). DOI: 10.4242/BalisageVol18.Caton01.

Abstract

Kiln, previously known as xMod, is an open source multi-platform framework for building and deploying complex websites whose source content is primarily in TEI/XML. It brings together various independent software components into an integrated whole that provides the infrastructure and base functionality for such sites. Separation of roles is central to Kiln's design, allowing people with different backgrounds, knowledge and skills to work simultaneously on the same project without interfering with one another's work. Developed and maintained at King's College London it has been used to generate more than 50 websites for digital humanities research projects which have very different source materials and customised functionality.

Table of Contents

Overview
Origins of Kiln
Kiln - the principle components
Kiln - as the user sees it
Kiln's templating system
Kiln introspection
RDF / Linked Open Data
Future for Kiln

Overview

Kiln[1], previously known as xMod,[2] is an open source multi-platform framework for building and deploying complex websites whose source content is primarily in TEI/XML. It brings together various independent software components into an integrated whole that provides the infrastructure and base functionality for such sites. Kiln has two competing design goals: to support the development of unique, complex web applications; and to provide an out-of-the-box system suitable for a single non-technical person to publish a TEI-based site. The former requires the customisability of every default component and the flexibility to integrate external components as necessary; the latter requires a large amount of built-in behaviour that can be easily tweaked in isolation, and excellent documentation. Kiln's documentation includes a tutorial showing how to customise each of the major elements of a site, as required beyond the provided defaults. Separation of roles is central to Kiln's design, allowing people with different backgrounds, knowledge, and skills to work simultaneously on the same project without interfering with one another's work.

Kiln is the latest iteration of work begun by a team at the Centre for Computing in the Humanities (CCH) - later the Department of Digital Humanities (DDH) - at King's College, London (KCL). Further development and maintenance of Kiln is now under the auspices of the recently-formed King's Digital Laboratory at KCL. Over the past years and over several versions, Kiln has been used to generate more than 50 websites for digital humanities research projects[3] which have very different source materials and customised functionality.

Origins of Kiln

Kiln originated at CCH around 2004 as a framework called xMod. CCH was collaborating with academic partners in text-based projects where primary sources were encoded using markup from the TEI Guidelines. From this work three things became clear:

1. Even for relatively simple, straightforward digital resources academics needed to come to CCH/DDH to have the resource built.
2. Multiple projects shared a core set of requirements.
3. In most cases, as well as the core set of requirements projects also had their own very particular and often quite complex needs.

And from them arose corresponding needs:

1. The need to give non-technical people a way to set up a basic digital resource that allowed web page display of XML-encoded source files.

2. The need to set up for ourselves a quick, dependable, consistent way of getting the core requirements dealt with to maximize time available for the project-specific work.
3. The need to be able to meet the particular requirements while still using the shared approach to basics.

Those needs pointed towards the best solution being a framework that enables a phased approach, where the initial phase involves quickly and easily setting up a basic digital resource which displays texts and offers basic browse and search functionality. Subsequent phases could involve any or all of the following: customizing the look and feel; expanding the browse and search capability; integrating with other things to create a larger whole (eg. having a CMS front end). This approach avoids making users choose between "simple" and "complex" versions of a framework.

Kiln - the principle components

Architecture: Figure 1 - Kiln Architecture

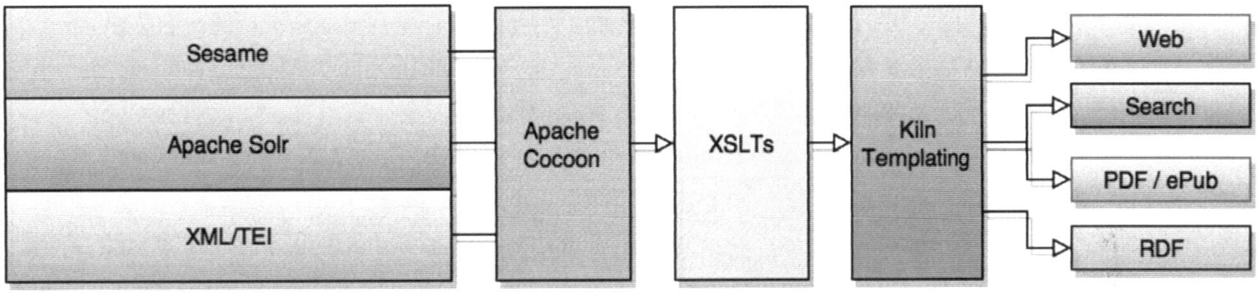

Kiln has been developed around the concept of the separation of roles, allowing people with different backgrounds, knowledge and skills to work simultaneously on the same project without overriding each other's work. The parts of the system used by developers, designers and content editors are distinct; further, the use of a version control system makes it simpler and safer for multiple people with the same role to work independently and cooperatively.

Given the needs we described above, Apache Cocoon[4] is a natural choice to sit at the heart of Kiln because the Cocoon sitemap+pipeline system is very flexible and powerful. At the basic level it is easy to create default paths and behaviours which are available to users after a few simple steps, thus meeting needs (1) and (2). Then, if desired, we can set up processing sequences of increasing complexity and/or granularity which supplement the defaults rather than replacing them - thereby satisfying need (3).

The Solr search platform[5] is a good complement to Cocoon. At the basic level we can have simple indexing pipeline to provide a free text search facility (see next section, below). As our needs become more complex - when, for example, we might want to incorporate into the index data from non-primary sources such as authority files, bibliographies, and so on - we can use Cocoon's aggregation mechanism to bring the disparate sources together and channel them into a single indexing transformation. By using internal Cocoon URLs we can pre-process some of the secondary sources and channel the output into the aggregation. And because Solr has numerous faceting features built-in we can easily add faceted browsing functionality to the resource; indeed this step is so straightforward that even a site admin with relatively modest technical knowledge can implement it.

Earlier versions of Kiln - then named xMod - used XML databases such as eXist for storing and indexing structured textual data and queried the databases using XQuery requests. Perfomance issues with XML databases led to our adopting Solr and since then we have had no compelling use case for XQuery so it is not included in the 'off-the-shelf' Kiln package.

Kiln comes bundled with the Jetty web application server[6] thus allowing Kiln to be a completely standalone application (beyond the user having the Java language installed on their machine). For a larger-scale production environment it is also easy to install Kiln as a WAR in, for example, an Apache Tomcat[7] setup.

The last main component of Kiln is the Sesame RDF framework[8], about our use of which we say more below.

One small convenience which this component set offers is that the parts that a user with limited technical knowledge might want to tinker with - ie. Cocoon sitemaps; Solr schema; XSLT stylesheets - are all in XML and the user is at least likely to be familiar and comfortable with its syntax and rules (assuming they are also responsible for the TEI content files).

Kiln - as the user sees it

After dowloading it or cloning it from GitHub, the user can start Kiln from the command line with ./build.sh (there is a .bat version for Windows) to use the built-in Jetty server or alternatively can associate it with an existing Tomcat server. The default port is 9999 and on going there the user will see the default home page (Figure 2). Obviously this is intended to serve only as a place holder until the user 'finds their feet' and feels confident enough to begin shaping the site themselves. To that end the page offers suggestions about next steps and has a link to the online documentation which includes a tutorial that walks users through initial setup and common tasks.

Users can see a barebones display of their XML texts simply by adding them under ROOT/ as content/xml /tei/*.xml. The 'Texts' link which is already present in the navigation bar brings up an index list of files available, showing for each file some simple metadata extracted as part of the pipeline processing for the 'Texts' URL. This is default behaviour so the index list is always current without the user having to restart the server.

Welcome: Figure 2 - Kiln default home page

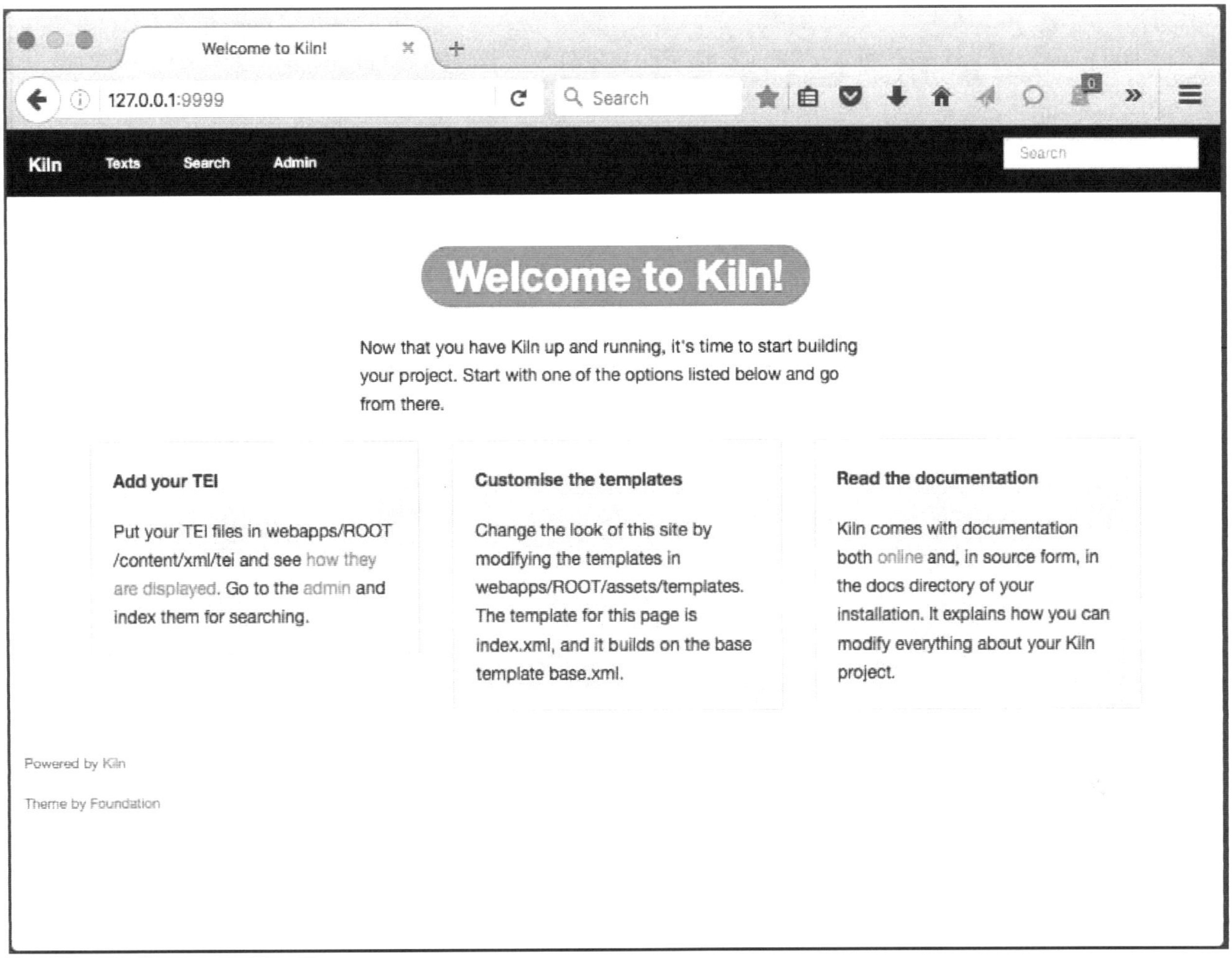

Kiln's default home page offers suggestions as to what the user should do next.

The most common need users have after being able to view their texts is for search capability. To enable this users go to the Admin page where a button lets the user run a Solr indexing process (Figure 3); when complete the user can perform simple text searches over the XML files.

Admin: Figure 3 - Kiln admin page

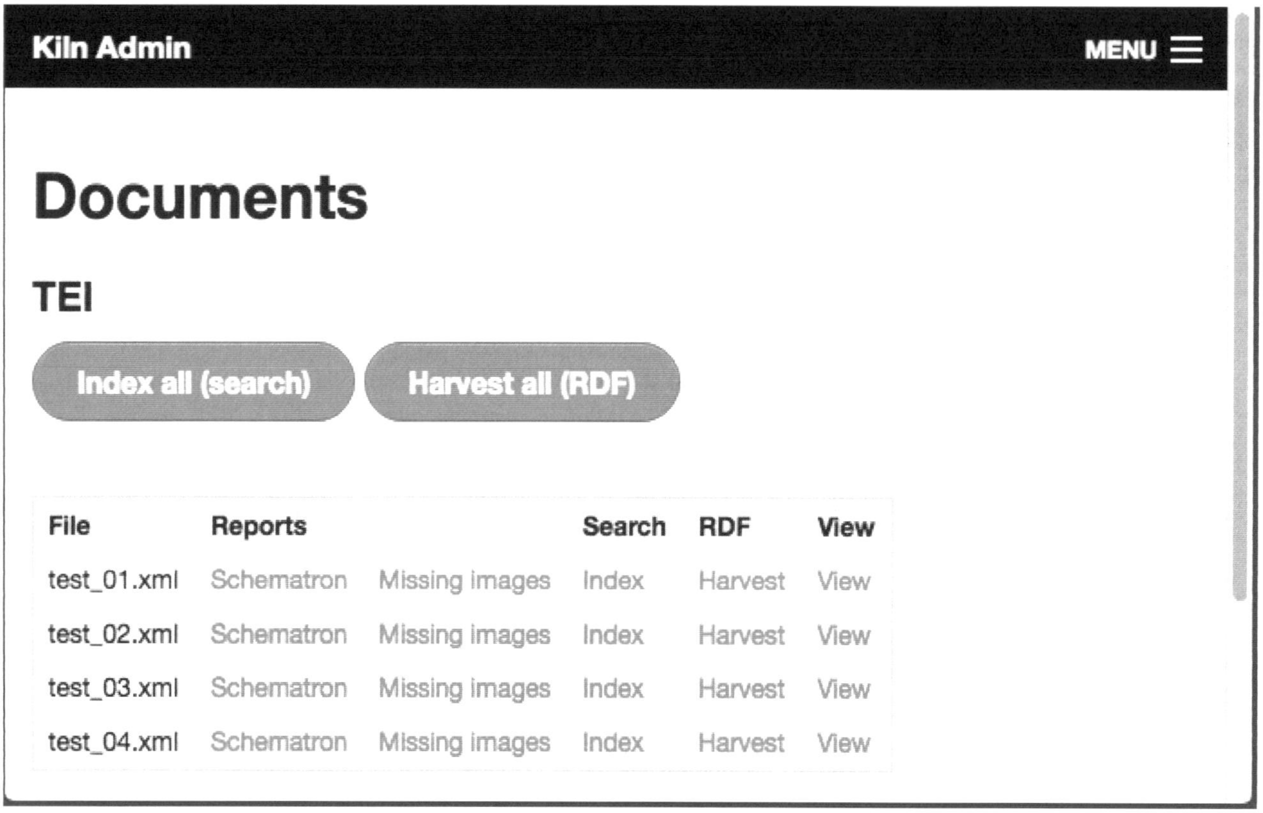

Kiln's admin page allows users to perform basic content processing operations.

Beyond this point a user wanting more advanced features such as faceted browsing will have to start editing application files. While the documentation provides guidance and the steps are not particularly complex, we do expect the user here to be at least comfortable with XML configuration files and XSLT stylesheets.

Kiln's templating system

Where TEI-encoded XML files constitute the main source content, an XSLT transformation remains the crucial gateway through which content must pass as it is fetched from the back end to be displayed on the front end. The approach we adopt to this part of the site workings is guided by the needs outline earlier. Ideally:

- It should be clear to non-technical users how displays are assembled.
- There are commonly required types of displays, so these should be 'pre-assembled' and offered by default.
- We also want to be able to adapt/add to/replace defaults to provide project-specific displays.

In addition to the desiderata just listed, we know that very often the person with the skills to write templates that find and handle parts of the source XML is not the person with the skills to organise the output into a functional, ergonomic, and aesthetically pleasing display - so we want our approach to allow for that. As far as is possible the XSLT specialist and the UI/UX specialist should be able to do their respective work concurrently and independently. Kiln handles these concerns by using a distinctive XSLT-based templating system. To show how this system works we'll follow a request for an XML source file to display as an HTML page.

- A request for texts/**.html goes to ROOT/sitemaps/main.xmap, is matched by a template.

- That template:
    - Firstly, creates an aggregate, which includes this: <map:part label="tei" src="cocoon://internal/tei/preprocess/{1}.xml" />
        - That preprocess call runs the XML through two stylesheets under **ROOT/kiln /stylesheets/tei** with the aim of identifying some known potentially troublesome features in the source XML and 'preparing the ground' for the final display stylesheet to deal with them.
            - One aggregates the content of div elements that are linked via "next" and "prev" attributes. Supposing an input markup structure like so:

              ```
              <body> <div xml:id="div_1" next="#div_2"> <p>content of div 1</p>
              </div> <div xml:id="incidental"> <p>intervening unwanted
              content</p> </div> <div xml:id="div_2" prev="#div_1"> <p>content
              of div 2 that continues div 1</p> </div> </body>
              ```

              the output structure would be:

              ```
              <body> <div xml:id="div_1" next="#div_2"> <p>content of div 1</p>
              <anchor xml:id="div_2"/> <p>content of div 2</p> </div> <div
              xml:id="incidental"> <p>intervening unwanted content</p> </div>
              </body>
              ```
            - The other moves pagebreak markers that occur in certain structural contexts into a different structural context (to stop what should be a single block display being broken up); and adds some kiln-namespaced attributes:
                - To block level elements saying whether or not they contain only inline material.
                - To link elements saying whether or not they are nested inside another link element.

              These attributes allow for allocation of CSS class markers that will help adjust the display formatting according to context.
    - Secondly, runs a transform on the aggregate with this call: <map:transform src="cocoon://_internal/template/tei.xsl" />. The important thing here is that tei.xsl *does not exist as an actual stylesheet*. Instead, the cocoon URL pattern is matched in **/ROOT/kiln/sitemaps/main.xmap** as "_internal/template/**.xsl" by a template which:
        1. Looks for a template XML file which matches the wildcard value (in this case it would be "tei", so it looks for tei.xml).
        2. On the template XML file it runs: <map:transform type="xinclude"/> to grab anything referenced with an xinclude. So for example it acts on <xi:include href="base.xml"/> to bring in a template file which sets up the overall default HTML page framework.
        3. Then on the template XML file it runs: <map:transform src="../stylesheets /template/inherit-template.xsl" />; inherit-template.xsl is an actual stylesheet which creates what is effectively a virtual stylesheet as its output - and that output functions as 'tei.xsl', applies the templates defined within itself, and thereby completes the transformation call that originated with <map:transform src="cocoon://_internal/template/tei.xsl"/>.
- Finally the output from 'tei.xsl' is serialized as HTML by a <map:serialize/> instruction. (Note that the default type of serializer is set to be HTML in sitemap.xmap, so no @type is specified.)

The processing sequence outlined above allows a designer to shape the structure of output web pages by putting HTML directly into the template XML files. They don't need to know anything about writing XSLT templates because they never need to edit an XSLT stylesheet. An inheritance system based on named blocks means all parts of a page can be customized and at different levels of granularity. Each template file has as its first element `<kiln:parent>`, with an XInclude child that brings in the base.xml template. This template is an hierarchical structure of named `<kiln:block>` elements which by itself supplies all the necessary elements of a web page. The idea is that the calling template (tei.xml in our example) declares named `<kiln:block>`s each of which overrides part-or-all of the equivalent `<kiln:block>` in base.xml. If the named `<kiln:block>` in the calling template has a `<kiln:super>`as its first child element, that imports all the content and functionality of the corresponding named block in the parent template. The user can then add elements according to what they wish to override from the parent. With this templating mechanism overriding can occur from a very granular level all the way up to the top-level `<kiln:block name="html">`. This means the user can easily create a page that looks different in almost every way from their other pages but that is still a regular page as far as the framework is concerned.

Kiln introspection

Another distinctive feature of Kiln is the ability to see the back end workings via the front end. Browser tools such as Firebug can give a lot of information about the current HTML page but do not usually reveal *how the page got that way*. Non-technical site owners normally have only a limited grasp of the back-end workings, and if the site is complex with multiple sitemap/pipeline files in play then even developers can have a tedious time identifying templates and stylesheets responsible for producing a particular page. As a development and debugging aid Kiln allows users to view relevant aspects of the processing mechanism via three different access routes:

- **Match for URL** - in a search text field the user specifies a root-relative URL from the site - eg. text/myfile.html - and the search returns the associated sitemap template
- **Match by ID** - the user is given a list of sitemap template identifier strings - eg. "local-tei-display-html" - and clicks on the name to see the template
- **Templates by file name** - the user is given a list of XML template files - eg. tei.xml - and can click on a link to see (via *view source*) the relevant XSLT stylesheet

RDF / Linked Open Data

Kiln includes the Sesame [9] framework for processing and handling RDF data. The framework is composed of two web applications, a server web application (openrdf-sesame) to store, parse and infer over RDF data, and a client web application (openrdf-workbench) to make queries over the data.

Sesame is built into Kiln via a set of Cocoon pipelines. By default there are pipelines for generating and adding RDF to the Sesame store, and pipelines for making SPARQL queries, in the sitemap file `ROOT/sitemaps/rdf.xmap`, which makes use of the basic operations - to add, remove, and query the triple store - defined in the internal sitemap `kiln/sitemaps/sesame.xmap`. Because the RDF requirements are very distinct across different projects, the default XSLT for adding content to the triple store is basically a placeholder meant to be extended and customised as required. The Kiln tutorial[10] includes a sample XSLT for converting TEI documents into RDF statements, and that can be used as a guide for further customisation work.

The main reasons to include a RDF framework with Kiln were to promote the publishing of linked data and also to increase the interoperability between the projects implemented with Kiln.

Future for Kiln

When CCH staff first began to shape xMod, they did so to meet specific needs which they felt were not being met by any free, open-source XML-to-webpage application available at the time. For the technically competent willing to 'get their hands dirty' on the server side there was Apache's AxKit[11], but this mod_perl module was not designed with convenience for non-specialists in mind (see, for example, Eric Morgan's account of trying to use it in Morgan 2005.) The most similar framework in the digital humanities field - the California Digital Library's eXtensible Text Framework (XTF)[12] was equally in its infancy at the time. Other existing frameworks such as TUSTEP ("TUebingen System of Text Processing Programs")[13] were more specialist in focus - designed to help scholarly editors produce editions - and without the same concern for enabling a website from XML-encoded source files. Today the landscape is somewhat different, with more applications available that are designed and documented with the non-technical user in mind.[14]

Most of the development work that produced Kiln in its current form was done via grant funding that ended two years ago. However, KDL still allocates time to maintain and further develop Kiln. Plans for the future include the possibility of a replacement for Cocoon, due to the lack of active development in Cocoon and also the direction that Cocoon is currently heading - its build process has become a lot more complicated with the later versions and it would not be possible to package a default version to be used in Kiln without off-loading technical work to the users. One possible future step would involve using XProc to handle the XML pipeline operations currently performed by Cocoon, but this would require an extensive codebase change for which (in the immediate future at least) KDL does not have resources to spare.[15] Another thing we would like to explore is adding modular extensions that could be easily 'made live' by the user and that would orient the functionality towards a particular content type, for example source files encoded according to the EpiDoc[16] guidelines. Tighter integration out-of-the-box with CMS frameworks is also a desideratum, as most project websites involve information pages, image galleries, etc. that are often more conveniently handled by such frameworks. Whatever is to come in the future, Kiln remains the most important tool that KDL uses to build XML-based online resources.

References

[Morgan 2005] Morgan, Eric Leese. "Creating and managing XML with open-source software" Library Hi Tech, Vol. 23 Iss: 4, pp.526 - 540. doi:10.1108/07378830510636328

---

[1] http://kcl-ddh.github.io/kiln/

[2] The name change reflected a major rewrite of the code. 'Kiln" was chosen to call to mind a container into which 'raw' source materials go and from which, after processing, 'finished' materials emerge.

[3] A list of some of these projects is available at http://kiln.readthedocs.org/en/latest/projects.html. Note that due to the nature of humanities grant funding a majority of these project sites remain as they were at point of launch. KDL can undertake to keep sites running for an agreed period (usually five years from the end of thew funding period) and fix bugs if caused by system updates/upgrades, but upgrading a project site to use a later version of Kiln usually depends upon the project partners acquiring extra funding.

[4] http://cocoon.apache.org/2.1/

[5] http://lucene.apache.org/solr/

[6] http://www.eclipse.org/jetty/

[7] http://tomcat.apache.org/

[8] http://rdf4j.org/

[9] http://rdf4j.org/

[10] http://kiln.readthedocs.org/en/latest/tutorial.html#harvesting-rdf

[11] http://attic.apache.org/projects/axkit.html

[12] http://xtf.cdlib.org/

[13] http://www.tustep.uni-tuebingen.de/tustep_eng.html

[14] For example, <teiPublisher>, TEICHI, Edition Visualization Technology

[15] Kiln is, however, open source and interested parties are welcome to contribute to the codebase.

[16] https://sourceforge.net/p/epidoc/wiki/Home/

Author's keywords for this paper: Cocoon pipelines; templating; XSLT

Paul Caton
<paul.caton@kcl.ac.uk>
Research Analyst, King's Digital Laboratory
King's College, London

Paul Caton has worked in digital humanities since for two decades. Beginning as Electronic Publications Editor for the Women Writers Project he went on to hold posts with the TEXTE Project at the National University of Ireland, Galway and with the INKE Project at the University of Victoria in British Columbia before going to the Centre for Computing in the Humanities at King's College, London in 2010. Now a Research Analyst in the recently-formed King's Digital Laboratory he works on multiple projects in both analytical and development roles. His research interests include the representation of text by formal models and by markup languages; ontologies of personal relations; and models of transcription.

Miguel Vieira
<jose.m.vieira@kcl.ac.uk>
Software Engineer, King's Digital Laboratory
King's College, London

Miguel Vieira is Kiln project manager and one of the developers. He has worked in the digital humanities area as a developer/software engineer for more than ten years. He is currently a software engineer/technical coordinator at the recently-formed King's Digital Laboratory, where he is reponsible for the research projects technical architecture, and managing the development team. His research interests include analysing and modelling humanities and unstructured data, natural language processing, machine learning, data visualisation, and linked data.

Link to the Balisage Proceedings Home Page at http://www.balisage.net/Proceedings
Link to this paper (entry page with links) at http://www.balisage.net/Proceedings/vol18/html/Clark01/BalisageVol18-Clark01.html

XML In, Web Out: International Symposium on sub rosa XML

Proceedings

Meta(data)morphosis

Ashley M. Clark

Sarah Connell

XML In, Web Out: International Symposium on sub rosa XML
August 1, 2016

Copyright © Ashley M. Clark and Sarah Connell, 2016. Some rights reserved.

How to cite this paper

Clark, Ashley M., and Sarah Connell. "Meta(data)morphosis." Presented at XML In, Web Out: International Symposium on sub rosa XML, Washington, DC, August 1, 2016. In *Proceedings of XML In, Web Out: International Symposium on sub rosa XML*. Balisage Series on Markup Technologies, vol. 18 (2016). DOI: 10.4242/BalisageVol18.Clark01.

Abstract

This article offers a case study in the creation and metamorphosis of a corpus of transcriptions intended for web publication. It discusses a process for encoding, proofing, and publishing a collection of brief periodical documents (largely reviews) on the subject of authors published in the Women Writers Project's established Women Writers Online corpus, as part of an initiative investigating the transatlantic reception of early women's texts. Both encoding and publication in the initiative, Cultures of Reception, were driven by the particular characteristics of this collection and the importance of establishing links to the existing materials in Women Writers Online. This article discusses steps that the Cultures of Reception team took to prepare the encoded texts for publication—including development of a web-based tool systematizing human intervention—and then explains the goals and design of Women Writers in Review, the interface that is used to publish these texts.

Table of Contents

- Introduction
  - Context for Cultures of Reception
  - The First Phases
- Reports and Initial Cleanup
  - The Ill-formed Transcriptions
  - The Lack of Identifiers
  - The Inspecter
    - Formedness, Well-Done
    - Entity Recognition
  - The JSON-to-XML Migration
- Preparing for Publication
  - Building Entity Records
  - Creating Display Titles
  - Reconciling Inconsistencies

Women Writers in Review
Interface Goals
Infrastructural Design
In Conclusion: Metadata Narratives
Acknowledgments
Appendix A. Appendix A: Metadata Comparison between Women Writers Project Publications
Appendix B. Appendix B: Original JSON Keys
Appendix C. Appendix C: JSON to TEI

Introduction

The Cultures of Reception initiative offers a case study in the migration, normalization, enhancement, and transformation required to publish a set of TEI-encoded data. The initiative's corpus consists of almost 700 transcriptions demonstrating the cultural engagements and influences of women writers in the eighteenth and nineteenth centuries. The corpus is large enough and most of its transcriptions are short enough that publishing this corpus required prioritizing the use of data in aggregate over individual transcriptions. And, while the corpus is also small enough that it cannot be considered definitive, cleaning and enhancing the transcriptions' metadata enabled their publication in an interface that allows users to discover, to explore, and to make connections among a set of texts and authors that enact a key moment for women's participation in transatlantic print culture. The data enhancement and publication processes required, among other things, the migration of data from JavaScript Object Notation (JSON) to XML encoded following the Text Encoding Initiative (TEI)'s guidelines[1]; the rehabilitation of ill-formed transcriptions; the identification of entities such as people and literary works; the formalization of metadata associated with texts and publications; and, of course, the development of a web interface capable of accomplishing the project's goals for these materials.

The Women Writers Project (WWP)[2] began work on the Cultures of Reception initiative in 2010. To support research into the transatlantic reception and readership of early texts by women, the WWP transcribed close to 700 brief documents—such as literary reviews, publication announcements, textual excerpts, and subscription notices—published in Great Britain, Ireland, and America between 1770 and 1830. This paper focuses on the tasks which preceded and enabled the release of an exploratory web interface, Women Writers in Review,[3] which makes the Cultures of Reception corpus available for discovery and reading. As is evident in this project—in which transcriptions were created in one web interface, edited and transformed into well-formed XML through another interface, and then published through a third—the processes of authoring XML files for web publication and of developing web interfaces to publish XML files need not be entirely distinct; in fact, they can be productively linked. This paper discusses how, by focusing extensively on the corpus's metadata, we at the WWP managed the complexity of the Cultures of Reception source materials and addressed the need to create a publication platform in which even novice users can navigate these materials.

Context for Cultures of Reception

The Cultures of Reception corpus represents a major encoding and publication endeavor for the WWP—but it was produced in the context of a much longer established collection of TEI-encoded texts: Women Writers Online (WWO).[4] WWO is full-text collection of early women's writing in English; it includes transcriptions of texts written, translated by, or attributed to women, published between 1526 and

1850, and it has been central to the WWP's research output for close to thirty years. The various "reviews" (a term we have broadly defined to include not only reviews, but also publication notices, literary histories, and other texts discussing women's writing) that make up the Cultures of Reception corpus were selected because they respond to texts by authors who are published in WWO. Thus, while the two collections are distinct in their contents, encoding practices, and publication interfaces, they are closely linked to each other through their shared focus on a set of authors and texts.

Although both Cultures of Reception and WWO are TEI projects, their encoding practices differ significantly. The tagset for Cultures of Reception is fairly minimal, designed to capture basic document structures, significant renditional details, and the evidences of textual exchanges (such as quotations and references to titles) that are important for the project's concerns with early transatlantic review culture.[5] The WWO collection, by contrast, has a tagset that currently includes approximately 165 elements and that reflects decades[6] of development with a generically and chronologically diverse collection of texts. Finally, while the two interfaces will be linked extensively, their purposes and display needs are quite different. WWO is designed as a reading interface, making individual texts easy to locate and read online. Cultures of Reception places a high priority on aggregation; its texts are generally shorter than those in WWO and they are more likely to be discovered through their periodicals of publication or subject matter than by reviews' titles or authors. For this reason, Women Writers in Review (WWR), the web interface in which the Cultures of Reception collection is published,[7] foregrounds metadata much more than WWO does and fosters exploration by a wider range of facets.

The Cultures of Reception transcriptions require significantly more context to be useful and their metadata reflects that. Where each WWO text only needs to track information about the individual publication and its author(s), a Cultures of Reception review needs to track information about where the review was originally published, which publication was reviewed, which edition is likely to be the one reviewed, and which authors were mentioned. We also wanted the materials in Women Writers in Review to enrich the experience of reading the texts in Women Writers Online, linking between the two corpora as much as possible. See Appendix A for a tabular comparison of metadata captured in WWO versus in Cultures of Reception. While the complexity of the Reception data is specific to the project, we hope to demonstrate that our focus on metadata added a great deal of value to the web publication of our small- to mid-size corpus.

The First Phases

The initial phases of the Cultures of Reception initiative were completed between 2010 and 2013, during which time the Women Writers Project had its institutional home at Brown University. These phases included selecting, sourcing, and gathering data on the texts to be encoded; setting up a web interface connected to CouchDB[8] for a first pass of transcription and encoding; and performing a substantial amount of the encoding work itself. The WWP's project manager at that time, John Melson, took the lead in creating the transcription interface and gathering metadata on the reviews and periodical sources. The bulk of the transcription and encoding work was performed by the WWP's graduate and undergraduate student encoders.

Figure 1: The transcription interface

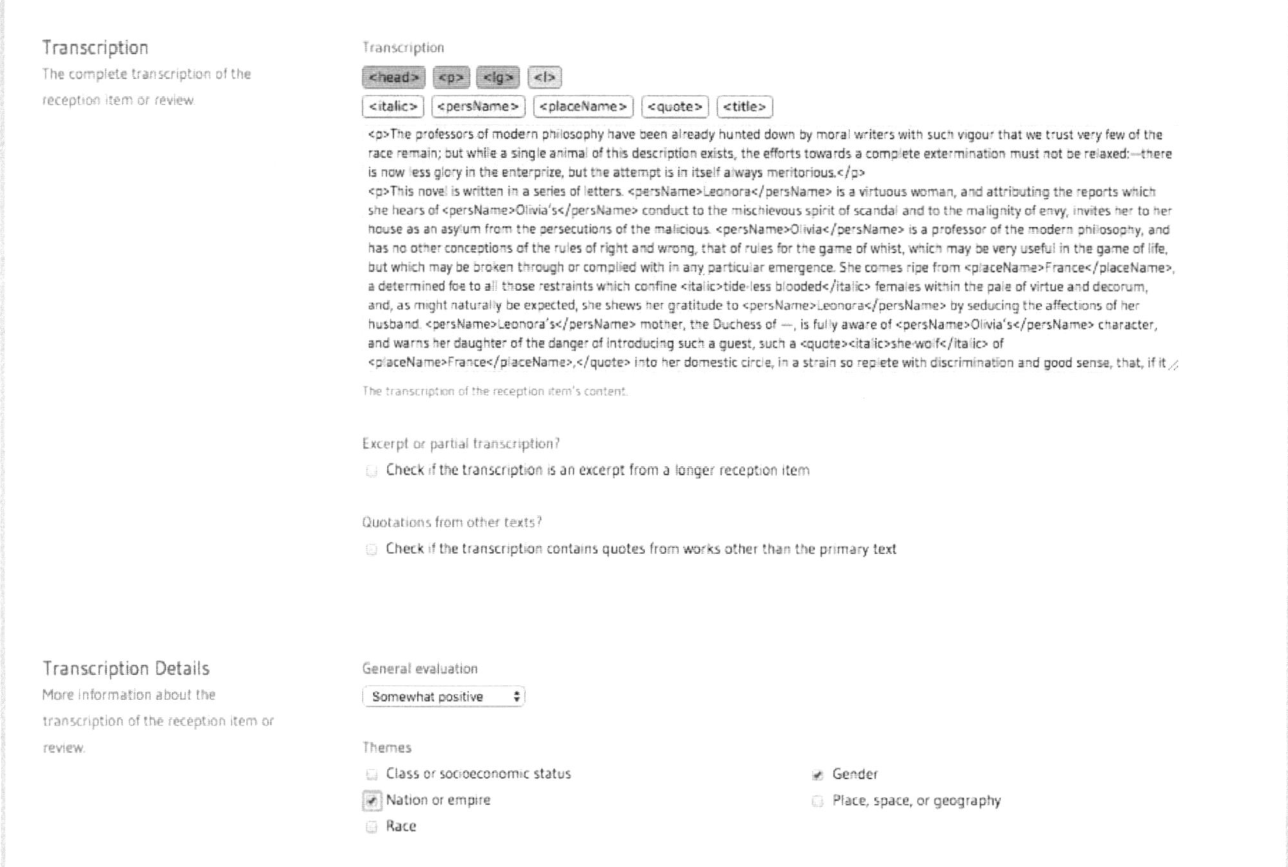

The transcription interface, showing an example review with buttons for entering markup and additional tagging through checkboxes and dropdowns.

It was after the WWP moved to Northeastern University in 2013 that this paper's authors became involved with the Cultures of Reception initiative. Sarah Connell, the WWP's current project manager, directed a team of graduate students as they continued encoding in the transcription interface and worked with Ashley Clark, the WWP's XML Applications Developer, on proofing the corpus and preparing the transcribed texts for web publication. In the sections that follow, we discuss the decisions that we made and the work that we performed after the first transcription phase had been completed and we began to focus extensively on publishing the collection.

Reports and Initial Cleanup

As transcription wrapped up, we began to take stock of the data stored in CouchDB as JSON objects.[9] We used XQuery to pull records from CouchDB's API. Examining the query results, we realized that we could not yet create accurate reports on the writers, works, and periodical sources represented in the database. Most of the JSON objects' values were inconsistently formatted and difficult to parse programmatically. From a human standpoint, the sheer volume of reviews in the corpus made it extremely difficult to find specific transcriptions. Browsing the list of records was overwhelming even for those who knew the project.

These first queries shaped the rest of the pre-publication phase by helping us to recognize that, in order to appeal to the casual user, the corpus needed to be browsable. Moreover, in order to appeal to the researcher, records needed to be discoverable. We decided that the best way forward would be to focus our pre-publication efforts on consolidating and normalizing metadata and determined that this would be easiest for our team to do once the corpus was migrated out of JSON and into XML.

First, however, we needed to take care of the transcriptions.

The Ill-formed Transcriptions

From the transcription interface, we knew we had 690 completed transcriptions stored in CouchDB. However, those transcriptions were stored as plain-text strings—pseudo-XML—in JSON.[10] While CouchDB has built-in methods of validating its databases using JavaScript, those methods could not tell us how many of those transcriptions could be exported as well-formed XML, much less valid TEI. Instead, we turned to an instance of eXist-DB[11] already running on the same server as CouchDB. We wrote an XQuery library to let eXist communicate with the Cultures of Reception database through CouchDB's API. Using that library, we attempted to serialize the JSON records as XML and save them into eXist. But, while CouchDB didn't care at all about the transcriptions' XML-esque pointy brackets, eXist cared a little too much. It refused to store ill-formed transcriptions as XML because, of course, they *weren't* XML. Forget running XSLT on the strings! A direct export to TEI was just not possible.

Figure 2: JSON record CouchDB

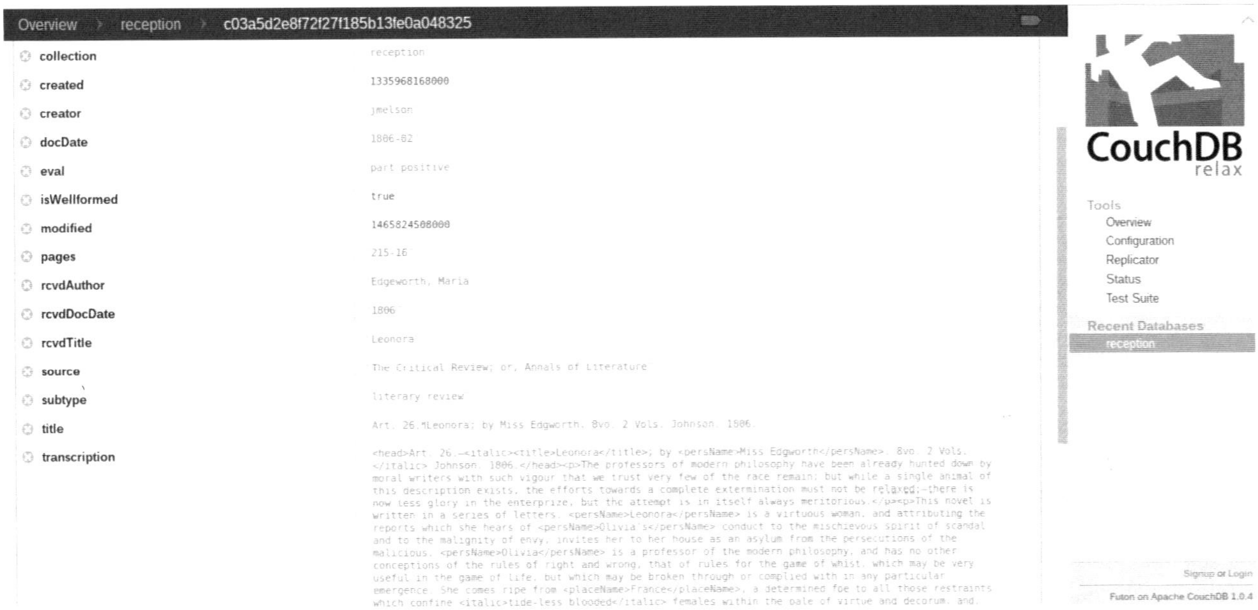

The same example review as it displays in CouchDB, showing both metadata fields and, in the transcription field, the XML-like strings.

Rather than strong-arming the JSON into a binary format, we decided to keep the transcribed reviews in CouchDB a little longer. eXist would serve as an intermediary for the transcriptions, running XQueries and storing XML reports on the CouchDB documents (rather than storing the documents themselves).

Figure 3: Ill-formed report-maker

```
reception.xql × | index.html × | couch.xql ×
(:~
 : Return a truncated report on each ill-formed transcription in CouchDB.
 :
 : @return XML
 :)
declare function cor:getIllformedTranscriptions() {
  let $docSeq := cor:getAll("_design/reception/_view/transcription", ())
  return
    for $record in $docSeq//item[@type eq "object"]
    return
      if ( $record//pair[@name eq "isWellformed"]/@type eq 'boolean' and $record//pair[@name eq "isWellformed"]/text() eq 'true' ) then
        ()
      else
        let $isWellformed := cor:isWellformed($record//pair[@name eq "transcription"])
        return
          if ( $isWellformed ) then
            ()
          else
            <corItem>
              <source>{ $record//pair[@name eq "source"]/text() }</source>
              <date when="{ $record//pair[@name eq "docDate"]/text() }"/>
              <rcvdAuthor>{ $record//pair[@name eq "rcvdAuthor"]/text() }</rcvdAuthor>
              <rcvdTitle>{ $record//pair[@name eq "rcvdTitle"]/text() }</rcvdTitle>
              <id>{ $record/pair[@name eq "id"]/text() }</id>
              <rev>{ $record/pair[@name eq "key"]/text() }</rev>
            </corItem>
};

(:~
```

A snippet from the XQuery library used to communicate with CouchDB. This function returns a sequence of records which fail a transcription well-formedness test.

Figure 4: Ill-formed XML report

```
reception.xql × | index.html × | couch.xql × | illformed-cor.xml ×
set  corItem  rcvdAuthor
<set xml:id="illformed-cor" toHTML="modules/illformed-cor.xq">
    <corItem>
        <source>The Augustan Review; a Monthly Production</source>
        <date when="1816-05"/>
        <rcvdAuthor>Morgan, Lady Sydney (Owenson)</rcvdAuthor>
        <rcvdTitle>O'Donnell: A National Tale</rcvdTitle>
        <id>c03a5d2e8f72f27f185b13fe0a0af25d</id>
        <rev>10-afe5b4d8ffcca75e172e2edfb3e96940</rev>
    </corItem>
    <corItem>
        <source>The New Annual Register, or General Repository of History, Politics, and Literature</source>
        <date when="1792"/>
        <rcvdAuthor>Smith, Charlotte (Turner)</rcvdAuthor>
        <rcvdTitle>Desmond</rcvdTitle>
        <id>c03a5d2e8f72f27f185b13fe0a112950</id>
        <rev>10-fae7730c430034f40d87e6416b8aa09a</rev>
    </corItem>
    <corItem>
        <source>The Critical Review; or, Annals of Literature</source>
        <date when="1817-05"/>
        <rcvdAuthor>Edgeworth, Maria</rcvdAuthor>
        <rcvdTitle>Comic Dramas, in Three Acts</rcvdTitle>
        <id>c03a5d2e8f72f27f185b13fe0a060532</id>
        <rev>11-108f31a61fda6434377e81f4264a0b35</rev>
    </corItem>
    <corItem>
        <source>The Critical Review; or, Annals of Literature</source>
        <date when="1797"/>
        <rcvdAuthor>Edgeworth, Maria</rcvdAuthor>
        <rcvdTitle>Letters for Literary Ladies. To Which Is Added, an Essay on the Noble Science of Self-Justification</rcvdTitle>
        <id>bee857503f04ddd247104bf6b602af26</id>
```

This report was used to identify ill-formed transcriptions for human intervention.

From the first of these reports, we learned that of the 690 transcriptions, 556 were ill-formed. After a moment of horror, we were relieved to discover that most of the 556 were actually just XML fragments; they only needed a wrapper element to be well-formed. That left us with 167 ill-formed transcriptions.

The Lack of Identifiers

Complicating this process, the records in CouchDB were not always consistent in terms of their metadata. There were no identifiers associated with the names of people, places, or publications. Instead, the transcription interface relied on alphabetical sorting of strings as a grouping mechanism. Because the names were typed in by hand, these fields varied in terms of punctuation, capitalization, and spelling—as one might expect—but also they also reflected variations in the amount of information and context included.

For example, one record might provide a reviewed author's maiden name ("Barbauld, Anna Laetitia (Aikin)") and another might not. Mary Robinson's works were listed under both her real name and her pseudonym, Horace Juvenal. And in the reviewed works, we found that two conflicting titles, *Harrington and Ormond, Tales* and *Harrington, a Tale; and Ormond, a Tale* were in fact *both* correct. The title had changed in a later edition.

The encoding interface was not flexible enough to handle the complex relationships among textual editions, or between two seemingly distinct persons. To address this limitation, some encoders wrote in-depth notes, attempting to capture context that would not fit in the HTML form.[12] The transcription interface did not encourage these contextual notes, though, and in any case, we couldn't reliably draw out those connections except with human intervention. Without identifiers to link key persons and publications, there was no ready way to programmatically categorize the 690 transcribed files by reviewed author or work. Additionally, it was not always clear which works referenced in the reviews corresponded to specific publications in Women Writers Online. We could not link transcriptions to each other, nor link out of the Reception project. We had a context problem. We needed...

The Inspecter

The Reception corpus was not small enough to allow human intervention on each and every item inside it, but the problems we faced were too complex for a purely programmatic approach. Instead, we used XPath and XQuery to create XML reports, then use a web interface—named "the Inspecter"[13]—to limit human intervention to situations requiring judgement calls, such as categorization or entity uniqueness. Any fixes would be ported back to CouchDB using its RESTful API.[14]

Formedness, Well-Done

For the ill-formed transcriptions, the XML report was simply a list of problematic records by their CouchDB identifier. The web interface was simple, too—an Ace editor[15] set up to parse an input field as XML. When the transcription was submitted, eXist would check it, only accepting the change if the XML fragment was well-formed.

Figure 5: Inspecter index page

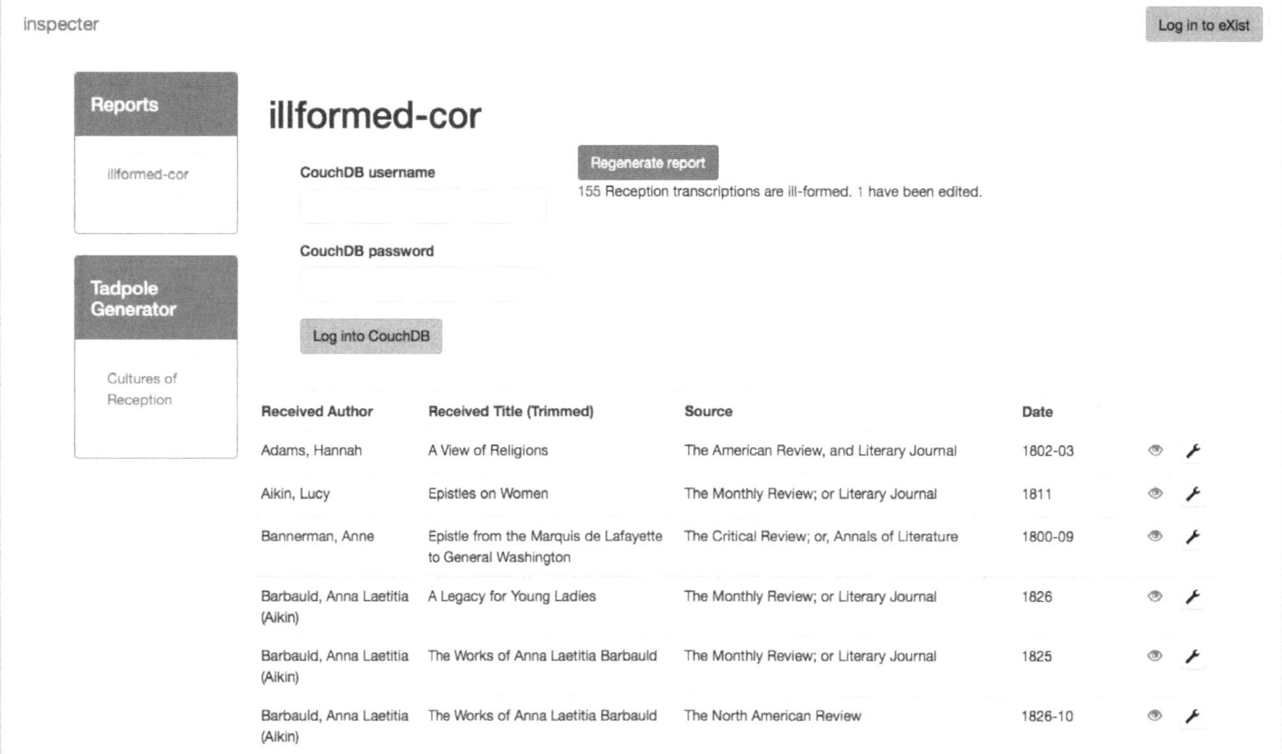

The index page of the ill-formedness Inspecter report.

Figure 6: Inspecter editing screen

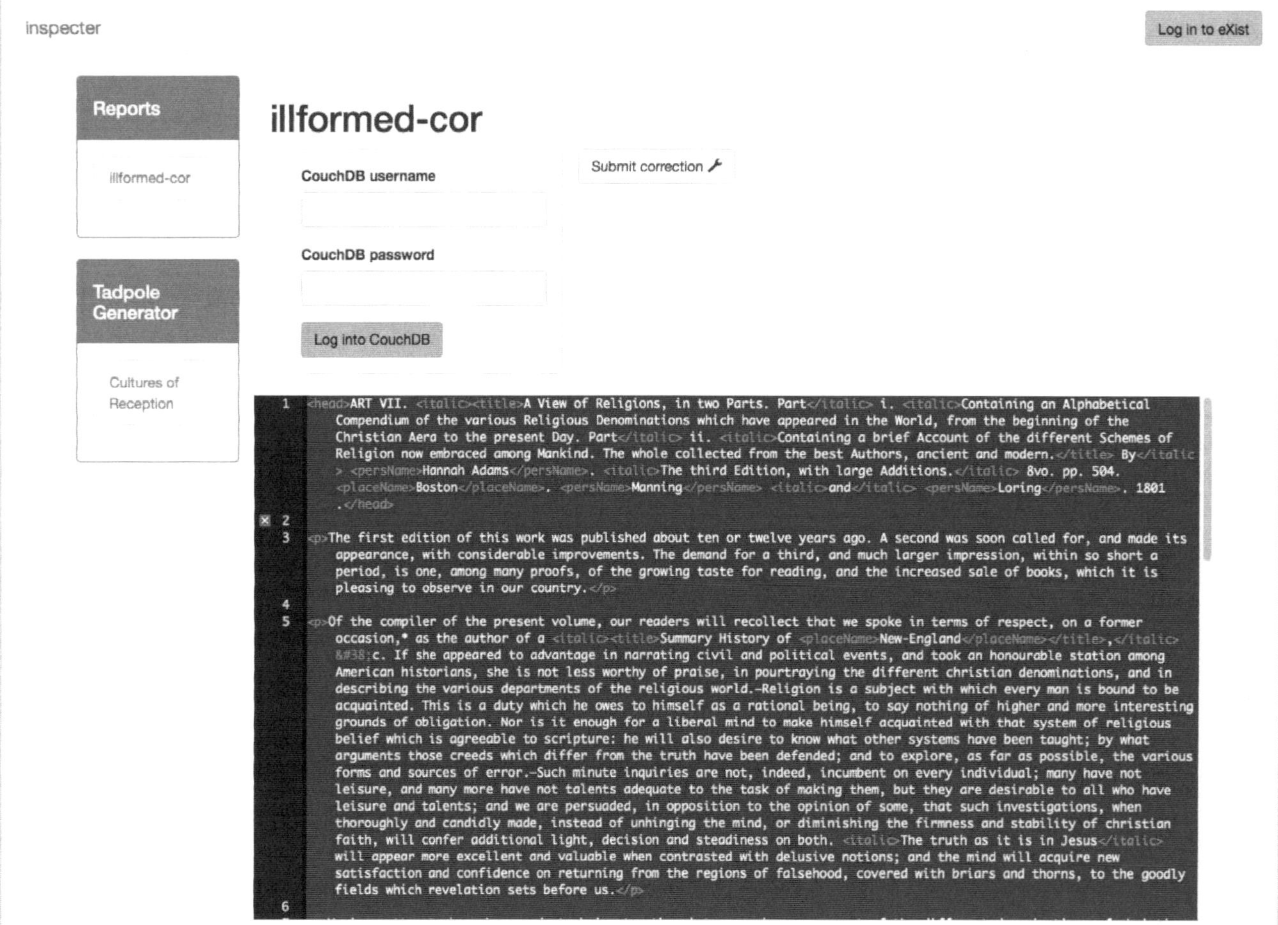

The editing screen of the ill-formedness report.

While Ace was an improvement over the original transcription interface, we quickly found that Ace's editing environment could barely keep up with the faux-XML. The editor could tell the data was ill-formed, but its error messages were not helpful in conveying *why*, nor in precisely locating problems within each document. Did an element lack a closing tag? Was there overlap? In cases where there was more than one ill-formedness error,[16] oXygen's interface proved more useful than Ace. By moving between oXygen and the Inspecter as the complexity of the errors demanded, we were able to resolve all but 20 of the 167 ill-formed files relatively quickly.

Entity Recognition

The second report was generated by identifying unique strings for both authors and the titles of works and then listing out corresponding reviews. The XQuery generating the report didn't even try to ignore punctuation or normalize misspellings, relying instead on the web interface to highlight subtle differences for the human reviewer. The displayed report sorted data by author name, then by work title, which made it easy to tell when authors' names or works' titles needed to be normalized, and allowed us to port the corrected string value back to the affected CouchDB records. It also provided the ability to link those reviewed works with an identifier for an edition in Women Writers Online, marking the transcriptions that did not have associated "TR numbers"[17] so that we could either add identifiers where they were missing, or mark reviewed works as not yet having entries in the WWP's records.

Figure 7: Missing TRs report

```
<set xml:id="missing-trs" toHTML="modules/missing-trs.xq">
  <!-- ... -->
  <rcvd author="Cushing, Eliza Lanesford">
    <work>
      <title>Saratoga; A Tale of the Revolution</title>
      <corItems>
        <corItem>
          <id>c03a5d2e8f72f27f185b13fe0a1f6b81</id>
          <key>2-891761cf27c81fc6446ad1cb20b8cbb7</key>
        </corItem>
      </corItems>
    </work>
    <work>
      <title>Saratoga; A Tale of the Revolution, in Two Volumes</title>
      <corItems>
        <corItem>
          <id>c03a5d2e8f72f27f185b13fe0a1f4e74</id>
          <key>5-cd0d37dff7de8b7c3574fe1787615bdb</key>
        </corItem>
        <corItem>
          <id>c03a5d2e8f72f27f185b13fe0a1f5cbe</id>
          <key>7-55180988969bfe1146de8c20723c3fcc</key>
        </corItem>
      </corItems>
    </work>
  </rcvd>
```

The XML report.

This Inspecter report was the first time we found the web interface to give us a greater degree of power than specialized software like oXygen. The Inspecter's strengths lie in: (1) reducing a complex dataset into a human-readable report, and (2) changing multiple records at once. The XML reports could be regenerated at the click of a button, so fixes were never held back by inaccurate reports.

However, the "Missing TRs" report also showed the value of simplicity. This report was used to trigger three separate data munging tasks:

1. normalizing reviewed author names,
2. normalizing reviewed work titles, and
3. linking reviewed works to their WWO versions.

Given the hidden interdependencies between tasks (in that normalization for authors and titles needed to be completed prior to entering links to WWO versions but the report did not enforce this order of completion), we initially struggled to find a good workflow for this report. Since then, each Inspecter report provides the structure to solve only one problem at a time.

The JSON-to-XML Migration

With the first two Inspecter reports completed, converting the CouchDB records into TEI-encoded XML was fairly simple. We used XQuery to request each transcribed, well-formed record in the CouchDB database, then turned that record into XML using the XQJSON library[18]. Each transcription was parsed as an XML fragment instead of a string representation. This XML representation of the JSON record was then transformed into TEI using XSLT, and stored in one of the WWP's eXist-DB instances. For simplicity's sake, the files were named by their CouchDB identifiers.[20] We then compressed the results into a ZIP file, and added the new files to a Subversion repository created and maintained by the Women Writers Project. Appendix B is a list of the JSON keys stored in CouchDB on export. Appendix C has screenshots of selections from the XSLT and XQuery files used to convert the JSON into TEI.

As for the 20 transcriptions with particularly thorny ill-formedness errors, the XQuery was used to transform all of the JSON data *except* the transcriptions. Each transcription was then treated as a string and wrapped in the `<body>`. The resultant files were also placed into the Subversion repository, in a directory for sequestered reviews.

We hope to rehabilitate these in the future, when there is more time to tackle the errors. In the meantime, the ill-formedness errors bothered our colleague Syd Bauman enough that he added attribute pointers, and split wrapper elements into empty ones.[21] The result is a collection of files in which the placement of the original encoding is preserved, and the files are not just recognizable to humans as XML, but *parsable* by XML processors.

Preparing for Publication

Building Entity Records

With the transcriptions in XML format and entities' names and titles normalized, we were able to query the data much more easily, which enabled us to discover that each transcription differed in how much data was included on any given entity. We could depend on the periodical title's presence, but not on the title under which the review was published. Some entries on periodicals included the publication place of the periodical, while others gave only the date.

One solution would have been to get compiled information for each entity and then propagate the condensed versions back to the reviews, as the Inspecter reports did to the records in CouchDB. This would have worked in the sense that every review would have access to the same information on its source periodicals and mentioned authors and works. But it would also retain the fragility of the CouchDB database—the reviews would easily get out of sync with each other as the collection continued to grow past publication.

Instead, we decided to create TEI files to house the canonical records of these entities. Previous WWP work had already established a research database of people and so we were able to make use of the WWP's "personography"[22] as context for any authors referenced in the reviews. For referenced works and periodicals, we used XQuery to create stub `<biblStruct>`s with only the distinct titles and newly-generated identifiers. After we created a TEI file for each set of bibliographic information, we used another XQuery to compile all the TEI elements associated with the `<title>`s, then save them to the new file, under the new identifier. We were then able to associate the reviews with identifier references to the canonical entries for their source periodicals and for any works mentioned.

The bibliography of mentioned works required a further step, since some reviews discussed different editions of the same work. We needed a way to show the relationship between different versions of the same work, not least because a goal of the project has been to investigate the international scope and cultural impact of women's writing. We settled on a loose correspondence of TEI bibliographic elements with Functional Requirements of Bibliographic Records (FRBR) entities.[23] The FRBR report conceptualizes intellectual products as four different types of entities: "works", "expressions", "manifestations", and "items". Works can have multiple expressions, and expressions can manifest in multiple ways:

Table I

FRBR Entity	Description	TEI Element
work	the text as a distinct artistic creation	`<biblStruct>`
expression	the text as created or interpreted in different ways	`<monogr>`
manifestation	the text as embodied in a published edition	`<imprint>`

We chose to identify works as having multiple expressions on the basis of on how much changed between different versions. For example, Hannah Adams wrote *A Summary History of New England*, and later reinterpreted her work for a younger audience: *An Abridgement of the History of New England for the Use of Young Persons*. We classified these two texts as expressions of the same work. Since the records were all in the same file and since intervention required a fair amount of bibliographic expertise, much of this identification was done by hand.

Figure 8: Bibliography sample

```xml
<biblStruct xml:id="CR0030" corresp="#frbr.work">
  <monogr corresp="#frbr.expression">
    <author>
      <persName ref="persons.xml#medgewort.onp">Edgeworth, Maria</persName>
    </author>
    <title type="main" subtype="display">Comic Dramas, in Three Acts</title>
    <respStmt>
      <resp>contributor</resp>
      <persName>Edgeworth, Richard Lovell</persName>
    </respStmt>
    <note>12mo. pp. 286</note>
    <imprint xml:id="CR0030.1" corresp="#frbr.manifestation">
      <publisher>
        <name>Hunter, R.</name>
      </publisher>
      <pubPlace>
        <placeName><settlement>London</settlement>, <country>England</country></placeName>
      </pubPlace>
      <date when="1817"/>
    </imprint>
    <imprint xml:id="CR0030.2" corresp="#frbr.manifestation">
      <publisher>
        <name>Wells and Lilly</name>
      </publisher>
      <pubPlace>
        <placeName><settlement>Boston</settlement>, <region>Massachusetts</region>, <country>United States of America</country></placeName>
      </pubPlace>
      <date when="1817"/>
    </imprint>
  </monogr>
</biblStruct>
```

A bibliography entry for Maria Edgeworth's *Comic Dramas*. The Cultures of Reception corpus includes references to a London edition (CR0030.1) and a Boston edition (CR0030.2), both of which roughly correspond to FRBR manifestations.

When we were satisfied with the bibliography of reviewed works, we used XQuery Update to replace the bibliographic metadata in each file with an identifier reference to the most applicable version of each work from the bibliography. This was done by comparing the `<biblStruct>` parts listed in each review with the condensed, canonical metadata in the bibliography. If the XQuery could not determine the most accurate FRBR entity, it used the work identifier with an attribute flag for low certainty. We were then able to search for that attribute and resolve the handful of problem cases.

Figure 9: Bibliography update script

```
xquery version "3.0";

declare namespace tei = "http://www.tei-c.org/ns/1.0";

declare variable $receivedOgraphy := doc('../../distribution/received-texts.xml');
declare variable $collection := collection('../../on_deck/?select=*.xml');
(: all imprint info: bee857503f04ddd247104bf6b60746de.xml :)
(: one date, no other imprint info: bee857503f04ddd247104bf6b601438f.xml :)
(: empty imprint: bee857503f04ddd247104bf6b60223d1.xml :)
(: a note in <relatedItem>: c03a5d2e8f72f27f185b13fe0a09c64a :)
(: low certainty on match (1 1 1): c03a5d2e8f72f27f185b13fe0a1cb578 :)
declare variable $docTest := doc('../../on_deck/c03a5d2e8f72f27f185b13fe0a09c64a.xml');

declare function local:match-cr-id($biblStruct as node()) {
  let $author := $biblStruct//tei:author[1]/(tei:name|tei:orgName|tei:persName)[1]/text()
  let $title := normalize-space($biblStruct//tei:title/text())
  let $publisher := $biblStruct//tei:publisher[1]/(tei:name|tei:orgName|tei:persName)/text()
  let $date := $biblStruct//tei:imprint/tei:date/@when
  let $pubPlace := $biblStruct//tei:pubPlace/tei:placeName[1]/text()
  let $monogrMatches := $receivedOgraphy//tei:monogr[normalize-space(descendant::tei:title) eq $title]
                                                    [descendant::tei:author/tei:persName eq $author]/tei:imprint
  let $evidence := if ( count($monogrMatches) ge 1 ) then
                      for $match in $monogrMatches
                      let $imprintSet :=
                        (
                          (
                            if ( $publisher ) then
                              $match/tei:publisher/tei:name[text() eq $publisher]
                            else ()
                          ),
                          (
                            if ( $pubPlace ) then
                              $match/tei:pubPlace/tei:placeName[text() eq $pubPlace]
                            else ()
                          ),
                          (
                            if ( $date ) then
                              $match/tei:date[@when eq $date]/data(@when)
                            else ()
                          )
                        )
                      return count($imprintSet)
                    else ()
  let $votedMostLikely := if ( empty($monogrMatches) ) then
                            ()
                          else if ( count($evidence) ge 1 ) then
                            for $position in index-of($evidence, max($evidence))
                            return $monogrMatches[$position]/ancestor-or-self::*[@xml:id][1]/data(@xml:id)
                          else
                            $monogrMatches/ancestor-or-self::*[@xml:id][1]/data(@xml:id)
  return $votedMostLikely
};

for $file in $collection//tei:relatedItem
let $relatedItem := $file//tei:biblStruct
return
  if ( not(empty($relatedItem)) ) then
    let $cr := local:match-cr-id($relatedItem)
    let $ref := <ref xmlns="http://www.tei-c.org/ns/1.0" xmlns:xi="http://www.w3.org/2001/XInclude" target="received-texts.xml#{$cr[1]}">
                {
                  if ( count($cr) gt 1 ) then
                    attribute cert { "low" }
                  else ()
```

Part of the XQuery used to test for accurate work identifiers.

Creating Display Titles

Another bibliographic issue we had to address resulted from the fact that very few of the items we transcribed had either titles or identifiable authors.[24] And, even for those that did, we knew that users would be far more likely to look for items based on the works being reviewed or the source publications. That is, we expect that readers would be more interested in retrieving the *Edinburgh Magazine's* various articles on Maria Edgeworth than in searching for "Review of New Publications" or "To the Editors of the *Virginia Religious Magazine*" in particular. And so, we decided to label each review according to the information that would be most useful to readers: its date, the source in which it was published, and the author and work that are its primary subjects. For example: "1817-09: *The Edinburgh Magazine* on Edgeworth's *Comic Dramas*".

We also knew that we would want to allow sorting and retrieval by source, reviewed author, and reviewed work. However, many of the texts in the Reception corpus have very lengthy names, making them unwieldy for web display, and so it was necessary to create display versions of these titles. In the relevant bibliographies for reviewed texts and sources, we added a second `<title>` with a @type of "display" and decided on a shortened version of the title (for the rare cases where titles were short enough already, we instead added a @subtype of "display" to the `<title>`). For example, Hannah Adams's

> *A View of Religions, in two Parts. Part i. Containing an Alphabetical Compendium of the various Religious Denominations which have appeared in the World, from the beginning of the Christian Æra to the present Day. Part ii. Containing a brief Account of the different Schemes of Religion now embraced among Mankind. The whole collected from the best Authors, ancient and modern*

has a display title of *A View of Religions, in two Parts.*

Establishing these display titles ensured that the Women Writers in Review interface could substitute the shortened form when the work or periodical source is referenced in headings and lists of results. In turn, users of the Women Writers in Review interface can scan through the significant amount of metadata necessary to locate individual reviews—and search through the collection overall—efficiently and without having to parse verbose titles such as *La Belle Assemblée, or, Bell's Court and Fashionable Magazine Addressed Particularly to the Ladies.*

Reconciling Inconsistencies

Our data cleanup process also required that we address the inevitable encoding inconsistencies that arise in projects on this scale. One such issue was the encoding of notes, which were handled in a range of ways (often reflecting the amount of experience the encoder had with WWO encoding practices); some encoders were simply typing notes as content where they happened to appear in the text while others were using `<note>` either at the location of the note or in a separate `<div>` at the end of the text. Fortunately, once we had all of the reviews well-formed and added to version control, it was easy to locate and reconcile the different practices so that all notes could be encoded in `<note>` elements at the end of each review. We were similarly able to address the occasional cases in which encoders both used the `<quote>` element and also typed quotation marks directly into the text. In fact, we found that many of the consistency issues that were difficult to enforce in the transcription interface proved to be very simple fixes once we had the files in XML because they could be identified, located, and addressed globally.

Figure 10: Sample encoding of notes

An example of transcription footnotes.

Another inconsistency we reconciled was, in fact, planned as part of the encoding process. During the early stages of the project, the WWP had identified several key themes that we were interested in tracking across the corpus—including topics such as "Nation or empire", "Gender identities", and "Review culture". We also wanted encoders to add their own thematic keywords, reflecting the specific content of different reviews and capturing themes that we hadn't anticipated. And so, we ended up with a broad set of encoder-created tags, many of which were expressing essentially the same concepts in slightly different language. For example, one encoder might mark a review as discussing "Irish literature" while another might use "literature of Ireland". We consolidated variations in the keywords, taking note of which encoder-authored tags were appearing frequently. In this way, the review process was also a method for us to get a sense of the content and concerns of the corpus overall and to refine the list of corpus-wide thematic tags, which we expect will be one of the major ways that readers discover content in the Women Writers in Review interface.

Women Writers in Review

Interface Goals

We had several key goals in mind when designing the corpus's web presence: we wanted to make the materials easy to browse and search; we wanted to have linking among the reviews and to Women Writers Online; and we wanted to foster exploration of the materials *as* a corpus. These goals were in many ways driven by the transcribed texts themselves, which tend to be brief and are more likely to be of interest to users as they reveal information about other texts and the larger topic of transatlantic reception culture. Women Writers Online, by contrast, tends to treat each text on its own merits; accordingly, the WWO interface is designed to make it easy to find and read individual texts. We expect that users of Women Writers in Review will be asking questions such as: "How has Maria Gowen Brooks been reviewed in British and American periodicals?" or "What changes are evident in the *British Review* over time?" or "How did periodicals in this period discuss questions of women's authorship?" (rather than "Where is Margaret Cavendish's *The Blazing World*?"—a question that brings a great many readers to WWO).

That said, we also wanted to do justice to the very lively and interesting content of the reviews in presenting them to readers—we don't expect that many readers will go looking for the *British Review's* article on Maria Edgeworth's *Harrington and Ormond, Tales*, but once that reader has found the article, we want to be sure it is easy to read online, despite the fact that it is one of the longer reviews in the collection. We also wanted to foster continued discovery and exploration from each individual review. For example, if a reader lands on this article from the *British Review*, they could go on to explore other literary reviews, other items tagged as dealing with nation and empire, other articles from the *British Review*, other reviews of Maria Edgeworth in general or of *Harrington and Ormond* in particular—and so on. For this reason, it was important that Women Writers in Review present all of the metadata associated with these items in intuitive and clearly organized ways.

Infrastructural Design

The web application for Women Writers in Review makes use of BackboneJS[25] to interface with eXist's RESTXQ endpoint[26]—more specifically, with an XQuery designed to return JSON datasets and HTML representations of the corpus. The web application was built out while the TEI files were in constant flux from undergoing the normalization tasks noted above, but because we started with the RESTXQ API, the BackboneJS app always had the latest data from eXist. Additionally, within the eXist database, the transcription files are stored separately from the EXPath app. These abstractions allowed for flexibility in our workflows. An update to the API did not require all records to be saved back into eXist and an update to the transcriptions did not require the re-engineering of the BackboneJS app.

Figure 11: Women Writers in Review web components

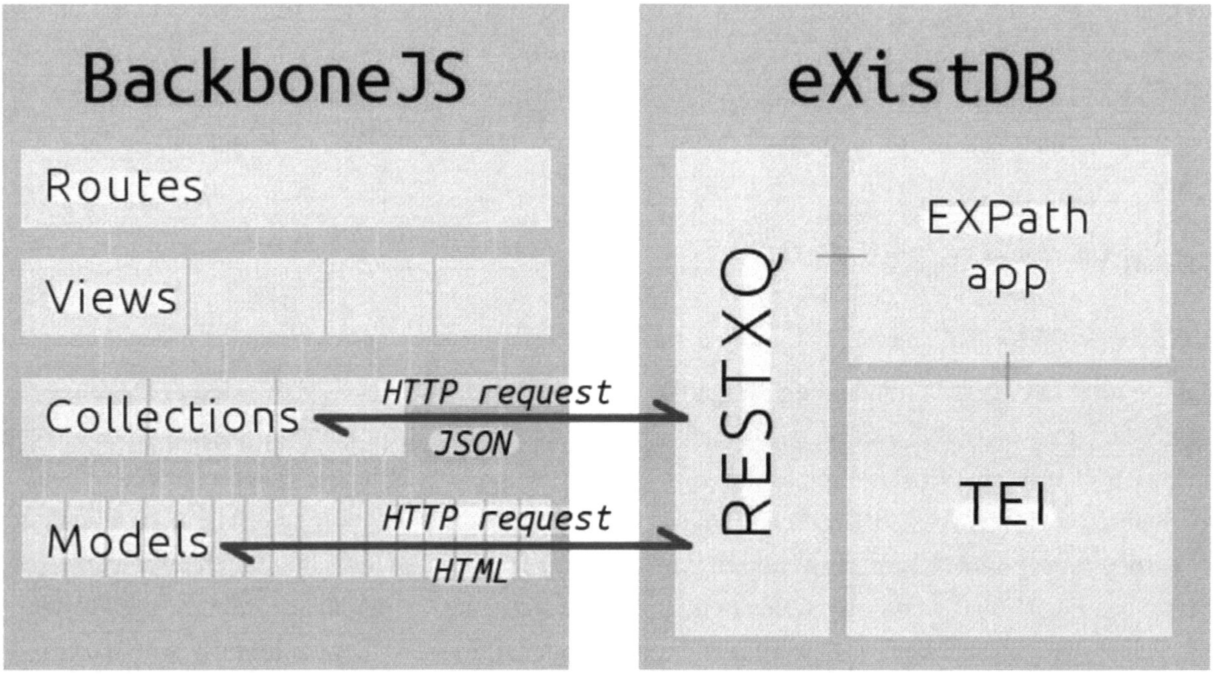

WWR makes use of BackboneJS to interface between the website reader and the XML corpus stored in an instance of eXistDB. However, because Backbone makes use of data compiled within eXist and served out using RESTXQ, researchers can also request the same data directly from eXistDB.

To accomplish the goals outlined above, we created a clean, simple reading interface using XSLT, and put much of our efforts into developing a series of landing pages, or pivot points, where users can view sets of items by reviewed author name, by reviewed work, by source, and by tags (such as format, genre, overall positive or negative evaluation, and thematic content). Each landing page is generated directly from the requested bibliographic or biographic canonical entry, using XSLT to create a representation of the appropriate context for that particular pivot. For example, the landing page for an author like Maria Edgeworth includes information on her pseudonym, her birth and death dates, her birth and death locations and the countries she resided in; it also links out to her entries in the Library of Congress Name Authority[27], the Virtual International Authority File[28], and WorldCat Identities[29]. Similarly, in addition to imprint data (such as publishers and publication dates and locations), reviewed works have a link to a version published in WWO, wherever WWO texts are available.[30]

Figure 12: WWR landing page sample

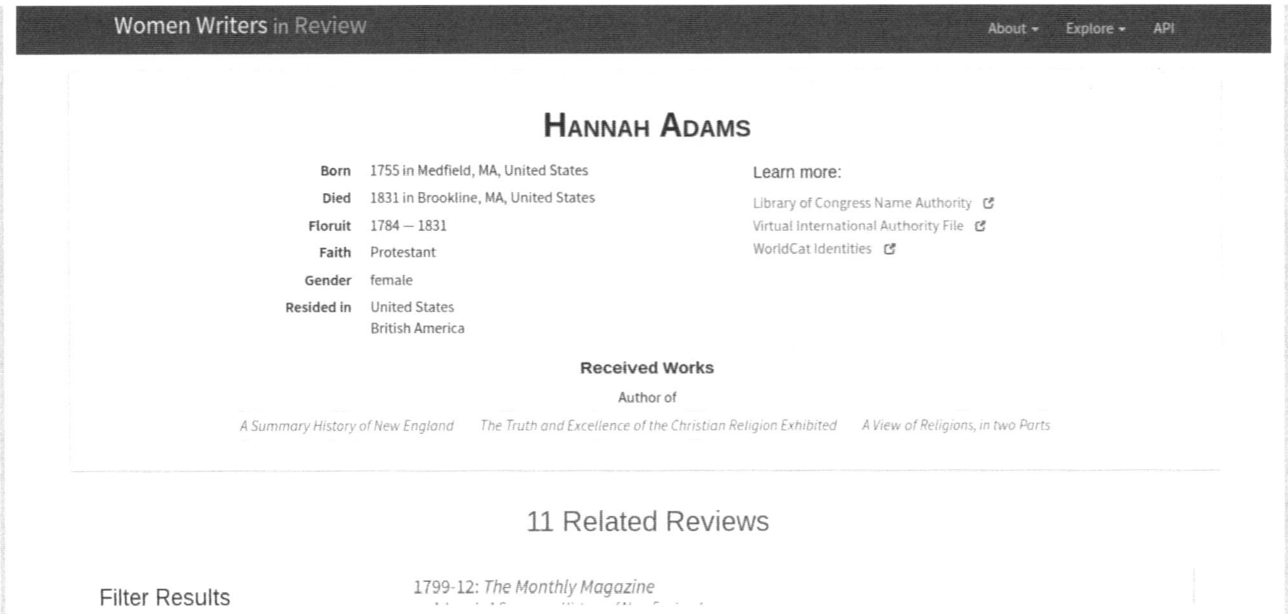

An example landing page for an author.

Landing pages also contain lists of reviews related to that particular pivot, and a facets sidebar. The sidebar is broken out by sources, tags, and mentioned authors and works. The sidebar distinguishes between facets that identify features of the result set, and those which can be used to reduce results to a subset. The latter are collapsed by default, while the former can be seen at a glance. For example, as one would expect, every item listed on the landing page for *The Literary Gazette; and Journal of Belles Lettres, Arts, Sciences, &c.* has that periodical listed as a source, so the "Source" facet in this case is used to indicate the number of results in the set, rather than to filter among those results. In a less predictable (and more interesting!) usage of facets for counting rather than filtering, the interface also shows that all results for this publication are articles with very positive reception of the primary author.

Figure 13: WWR results list sample

A sample result list on a landing page.

Figure 14: WWR faceting sample

An expanded facet category.

When users expand the actionable facets and select one, any items that do not match that facet are hidden, and items that do match are shown. Currently, only one facet can be selected at a time and the facets cannot be stacked or used to create a union of two subsets. As we continue creating features past initial publication, we plan to make the faceting system a better tool for querying, manipulating, or exploring aggregations of data.

Figure 15: WWR reading view sample

Women Writers in Review About Explore API

1806-02: *The Critical Review* on Edgeworth's *Leonora*

genre: literary review format: article or essay reception: somewhat positive

Unknown. "1806-02: *The Critical Review* on Edgeworth's *Leonora*." *Women Writers in Review*. Northeastern University Women Writers Project.

Source

Unknown. "Art. 26.—Leonora; by Miss Edgworth. 8vo. 2 Vols. Johnson. 1806." *The Critical Review; or, Annals of Literature*. Volume s3 7: pp. 215-16. 1806-02.

Author

Edgeworth, Maria

Work

Edgeworth, Maria. *Leonora*. London, England: 1806.

Art. 26.— *Leonora; by Miss Edgworth. 8vo. 2 Vols.* Johnson. 1806.

The professors of modern philosophy have been already hunted down by moral writers with such vigour that we trust very few of the race remain; but while a single animal of this description exists, the efforts towards a complete extermination must not be relaxed:—there is now less glory in the enterprize, but the attempt is in itself always meritorious.

This novel is written in a series of letters. Leonora is a virtuous woman, and attributing the reports which she hears of Olivia's conduct to the mischievous spirit of scandal and to the malignity of envy, invites her to her house as an asylum from the persecutions of the malicious. Olivia is a professor of the modern philosophy, and has no other conceptions of the rules of right and wrong, that of rules for the game of whist, which may be very useful in the game of life, but which may be broken through or complied with in any particular emergence. She comes ripe from France, a determined foe to all those restraints which confine *tide-less blooded* females within the pale of virtue and decorum, and, as might naturally be expected, she shews her gratitude to Leonora by seducing the affections of her husband. Leonora's mother, the Duchess of —, is fully aware of Olivia's character, and warns her daughter of the danger of introducing such a guest, such a "*she-wolf* of France," into her domestic circle, in a strain so replete with discrimination and good sense, that, if it were not too long for our purpose, we could with pleasure quote her whole first letter to her daughter.

Olivia's character is pourtrayed with a strong pencil, and the whole novel is written with great spirit. The sixth letter is an excellent specimen of moral reasoning.

The reading view for a sample review.

Both landing pages and reading views also include links within Women Writers in Review, to the landing pages for related entities or to sets of items with the same metadata. For example, one can link from the top of reading views to other reviews with the same tags as in the example above, which shows buttons linking to all items that are tagged as "literary review", "article or essay", and "somewhat positive". We hope that these connections among texts with shared characteristics will increase discoverability and make for an intuitive browsing experience.

In Conclusion: Metadata Narratives

The Cultures of Reception grant work has ended, but the Women Writers Project still has aspirations for improving Women Writers in Review. In the future, we want to use the refined metadata to offer readers more ways of exploring these reviews and of considering the corpus as a whole. We are currently adding visualizations showing trends in the corpus across time and location—such as positive and negative reviews of individual authors during the course of their writing careers—and we are working on making these visualizations themselves a mechanism that readers can use to explore the collection.

Figure 16: Sample visualization: evaluations over time

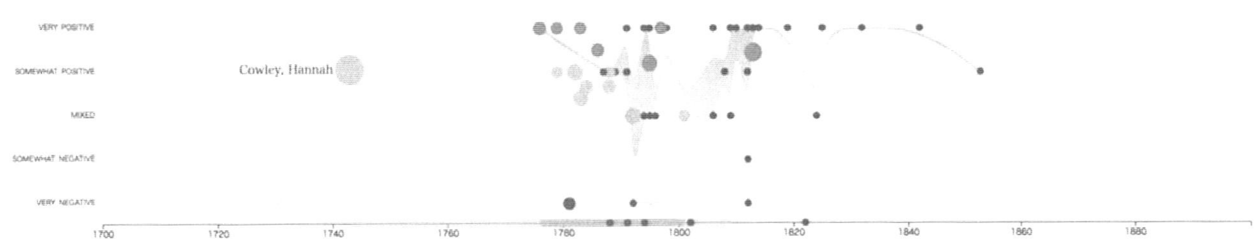

A prototype visualization for exploration of Women Writers in Review by positive and negative evaluations over time. Courtesy of Steven Braun.

We plan to make geographic information more visible—for example, plotting periodical sources and reviewed texts onto maps so that readers can investigate the roles that geographic space played in the circulation of these texts. While Women Writers in Review already has an API, we are in the process of expanding it and writing documentation to allow researchers to directly query the corpus and obtain results in JSON or XML.

Much of the framework is already in place for these goals. Metadata played a crucial role in the Cultures of Reception initiative, providing signposts from the earliest stages of transcription through the development of the Women Writers in Review publication interface. In the initial transcription phase, establishing a data capture mechanism that could accommodate our complex and highly structured textual and bibliographic data, while allowing a necessary degree of flexibility in the input, enabled us to complete a high volume of transcription work in a very short period of time.[31] Normalizing variations in that data early in the pre-publication process made it possible for us to map out and navigate the remaining data enhancement tasks, despite the diversity and size of the corpus. And it was the experience of navigating the XML files through their bibliographic and biographic data that inspired the design of Women Writers in Review. The result is a publication with a contextual foundation sturdy enough to build on. More importantly, we believe that foundation will empower users to read and to question, to explore and to discover, to experiment with and to theorize about the collection we have built.

Acknowledgments

The Cultures of Reception project was generously funded by a National Endowment for the Humanities Collaborative Research Grant.

The authors owe a considerable debt of gratitude to Julia Flanders, Syd Bauman, Steven Braun, John Melson, and the encoding staff at the WWP for their expertise and enthusiasm in developing the project.

Appendix A. Appendix A: Metadata Comparison between Women Writers Project Publications

All Women Writers Project initiatives include references to the same WWP-canonical personography—a TEI file with data on persons significant to the WWP. We at the WWP collect information on names (including birth names, married names, honorifics, pseudonyms, and name variants); geographic information (including birth and death locations as well as residences); dates (birth, death, and floruit); identifiers (including WWP and LCNA); and some biographic details (faith, marital status, parental status, and languages known). We also track authors' roles in the WWP's information systems—such as their roles as authors of texts in WWO, Women Writers in Context, and Women Writers in Review—and we keep open fields for notes, sources, and queries.

Table II

Identifiers are marked "ID", and identifier references are marked "IDREF".

	Women Writers Online	Women Writers in Review	
	transcription metadata	transcription metadata	canonical lists ('ographies)
WWP publication	file title	file title	
	publication information (publisher, date, place)	publication information (publisher, date, place)	
	file ID	file ID	
		CouchDB IDREF	
work attributed to a woman		IDREF(s) to any work reviewed, including the specific edition, if known	work ID(s)
	work title		work title(s), optionally including a shortened title suitable for web display
	contributor IDREF(s)		contributor IDREF(s)
	contributor name(s)		
	edition		edition(s), if known
	publication information (publisher, date, place)		publication information (publisher, date, place) for each known edition
	physical characteristics, such as the number of pages		
			Related WWO file IDREF, if one exists
source periodical		periodical IDREF	periodical ID
		review title	
		review author, if known	
		periodical title	periodical title(s), optionally including a shortened title suitable for web display
		publication date	publication date range, if known
		volume, issue	
			publication place
			publisher name(s), if known
			editor name(s), if known
			contributor name(s), if known
			politics, if known
			frequency of publication, if known
categories	work genre IDREF(s)	review genre IDREF(s)	
		review format IDREF	
		review theme IDREF(s)	
		IDREF of the evaluated tone the review takes to the main received work	
		keywords	
		Mentioned WWP author IDREF(s)	

Appendix B. Appendix B: Original JSON Keys

- title

- transcription
- isWellformed
- author
- editor
- pub[lisher]
- docDate
- volume
- issue
- pages
- source
- url
- wwp_tr
- rcvdTitle
- rcvdAuthor
- rcvdContributor
- rcvdEditor
- rcvdTranslator
- rcvdNotes
- rcvdEdition
- rcvdPub
- rcvdDocDate
- rcvdVolume
- rcvdIssue
- rcvdPages

Appendix C. Appendix C: JSON to TEI

Figure 17: Conversion step one: XQuery

reception.xql × | index.html × | export-item-to-tei.xq ×

```
xquery version "3.0";

import module namespace cor="http://wwp.northeastern.edu/reception/ns/couch" at "/db/apps/inspecter/modules/lib/couch.xql";
import module namespace xqjson="http://xqilla.sourceforge.net/lib/xqjson";
import module namespace sxn="http://exist-db.org/xquery/transform";

let $textsDir := "/db/reception-data/texts"
let $docSeq := cor:getAll("_design/reception/_view/transcription",())
(: Grab the IDs of records with well-formed transcriptions. :)
let $wfRecordIDs := $docSeq//item[@type eq "object"][descendant::pair[@name eq 'isWellformed'][@type eq 'boolean'][text() eq 'true']]/pair[@name eq 'id']
let $makeTEI := for $id in $wfRecordIDs
                let $json := cor:getReceptionDoc($id)
                let $allXML :=  <json type="object">
                                  { $json//pair[not(@name eq 'transcription')] }
                                  <pair name="transcription">
                                    { parse-xml-fragment($json//pair[@name eq 'transcription']/text()) }
                                  </pair>
                                </json>
                let $param := <parameters>
                                <param name="boilerplate-path" value="http://localhost:8080/exist/rest/reception-data/reception-boilerplate.xml"/>
                              </parameters>
                let $tei := sxn:transform($allXML,doc('/db/apps/reception/xslt/xqjson2tei.xsl'),$param)
                let $filename := concat(xs:string($id),'.xml')
                return xmldb:store($textsDir,$filename,$tei)
return $makeTEI
```

This XQuery transformed each well-formed CouchDB record into TEI using XSLT. The TEI was then stored in eXist.

Figure 18: Conversion step two: XSLT

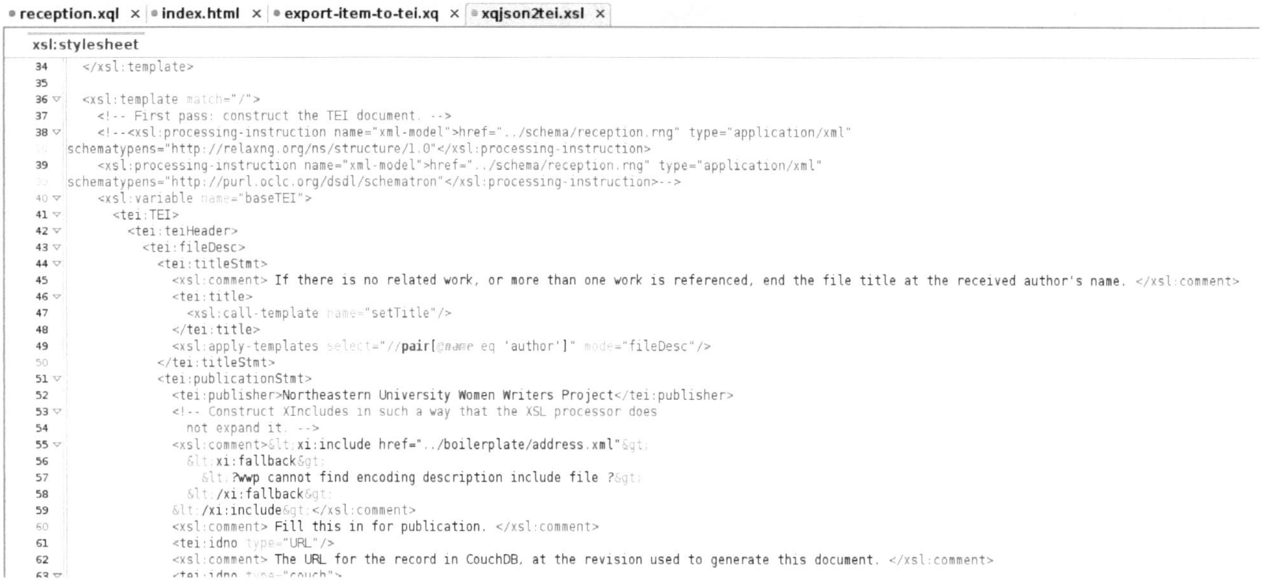

```
• reception.xql × • index.html × • export-item-to-tei.xq × • xqjson2tei.xsl ×
xsl:stylesheet
  </xsl:template>

  <xsl:template match="/">
    <!-- First pass: construct the TEI document. -->
    <!--<xsl:processing-instruction name="xml-model">href="../schema/reception.rng" type="application/xml"
schematypens="http://relaxng.org/ns/structure/1.0"</xsl:processing-instruction>
    <xsl:processing-instruction name="xml-model">href="../schema/reception.rng" type="application/xml"
schematypens="http://purl.oclc.org/dsdl/schematron"</xsl:processing-instruction>-->
    <xsl:variable name="baseTEI">
      <tei:TEI>
        <tei:teiHeader>
          <tei:fileDesc>
            <tei:titleStmt>
              <xsl:comment> If there is no related work, or more than one work is referenced, end the file title at the received author's name. </xsl:comment>
              <tei:title>
                <xsl:call-template name="setTitle"/>
              </tei:title>
              <xsl:apply-templates select="//pair[@name eq 'author']" mode="fileDesc"/>
            </tei:titleStmt>
            <tei:publicationStmt>
              <tei:publisher>Northeastern University Women Writers Project</tei:publisher>
              <!-- Construct XIncludes in such a way that the XSL processor does
                not expand it. -->
              <xsl:comment>&lt;xi:include href="../boilerplate/address.xml"&gt;
                &lt;xi:fallback&gt;
                  &lt;?wwp cannot find encoding description include file ?&gt;
                &lt;/xi:fallback&gt;
              &lt;/xi:include&gt;</xsl:comment>
              <xsl:comment> Fill this in for publication. </xsl:comment>
              <tei:idno type="URL"/>
              <xsl:comment> The URL for the record in CouchDB, at the revision used to generate this document. </xsl:comment>
              <tei:idno type="couch">
```

A snippet from the XSLT. The stylesheet's first pass constructed a TEI document from the XQJSON intermediate format. As templates were matched, some debugging elements were created. For example: `<DEBUG target="#cr.debug-andperson"/>` was created if a contributor field contained the word "and", suggesting that two `<persName>`s might be needed instead of one.

Figure 19: Conversion step three: XSLT

```
• reception.xql × • index.html × • export-item-to-tei.xq × • xqjson2tei.xsl ×
xsl:stylesheet  xsl:template
  <!-- cleanXML mode: remove TEI prefixes and apply debugging categories. -->

  <xsl:template match="/" mode="cleanXML">
    <xsl:variable name="debugCats">
      <xsl:apply-templates select="//DEBUG" mode="debugging"/>
      <!-- If there is no WWP-type identifier, add a debug category. -->
      <xsl:if test="not(//tei:idno[@type eq 'WWP'])">
        <xsl:element name="catRef" namespace="http://www.tei-c.org/ns/1.0">
          <xsl:attribute name="target" select="'#cr.debug-missingid'"/>
        </xsl:element>
      </xsl:if>
    </xsl:variable>
    <xsl:apply-templates mode="#current">
      <xsl:with-param name="extraCats" select="$debugCats" tunnel="yes"/>
    </xsl:apply-templates>
  </xsl:template>

  <xsl:template match="DEBUG" mode="cleanXML" priority="12"/>

  <!-- In debugging mode, turn all 'DEBUG' elements into catRefs. -->
  <xsl:template match="DEBUG" mode="debugging">
    <xsl:element name="catRef" namespace="http://www.tei-c.org/ns/1.0">
      <xsl:copy-of select="@target"/>
    </xsl:element>
  </xsl:template>
```

A snippet from the XSLT. With all templates applied to the pseudo-JSON record, the stylesheet then consolidated all debugging elements and turned them into TEI `<catRef>`s within the header. These could be found again using XPath.

---

[1] http://www.tei-c.org

[2] A long-term research and publication project focused on early women's writing in English.

http://wwp.northeastern.edu

[3] http://wwp.northeastern.edu/review/

[4] http://wwp.northeastern.edu/wwo/

[5] Restricting the tagset enabled the project to complete a relatively high volume of encoding work in a constrained period of time; it is possible that future research at the WWP will entail enriching the Cultures of Reception corpus with more detailed encoding.

[6] WWO itself was first published in 1999 and encoding work began years earlier.

[7] More information on Cultures of Reception and Women Writers in Review here: http://wwp.northeastern.edu/research/projects/reception/index.html

[8] A NoSQL database which stores JSON documents. https://couchdb.apache.org/

[9] JSON objects are unordered lists of keys and their associated values.

[10] The plain-text looked like XML in that it had pointy brackets and element-like structures, but it was not serialized as XML. Because it hadn't been serialized as XML, there was no guarantee that the text was hierarchical or had only one root element.

[11] An open source XML database. http://exist-db.org

[12] For example, one note on a text discussing Elizabeth Ogilvy Benger's *Poems on the Abolition of the Slave Trade* reads: "Elizabeth Benger is apparently only named in the work as E. Benger, and she is referred to as Mr. Benger throughout the review. There is an interesting footnote on the bottom right of page 104, which speculates that E. Benger might be a woman."

[13] The idea for the interface was conceived around Halloween. Its name combines "inspector" (for its task-based reports) with "specter" (for the ghostly way those reports were displayed: data unmoored from its context). In the future, the name will be changed to "inspectre" to better embody the pun.

[14] http://docs.couchdb.org/en/latest/intro/api.html

[15] AceJS is a JavaScript-based, embeddable code editor. https://ace.c9.io

[16] This was, unfortunately, common.

[17] The unique identifier for WWO texts ("TR" is short for "transcription").

[18] This helpful EXPath library[19] aids in JSON-XML translation, though conversion can certainly be accomplished using other methods. https://github.com/joewiz/xqjson

[19] XQuery functions packaged for easy installation and propagation. http://expath.org/spec/pkg

[20] CouchDB identifiers are long and not particularly human-readable, but they had the advantage of being unique. We later changed the filenames to use the primary reviewed author's surname, a key for the primary reviewed work, and a key for the periodical in which the review was published. This yielded filenames that were at least human-readable, though still lengthy.

[21] An unofficial lesson from this project: offending developers' sensibilities can be a positive force for change.

[22] A TEI file with structured data on persons.

[23] FRBR is recommendation by the International Federation of Library Associations and Institutions (IFLA). http://www.ifla.org/publications/functional-requirements-for-bibliographic-records

[24] In fact, all but a handful are either anonymous or pseudonymous.

[25] A model-view-controller library for creating web applications in JavaScript. http://backbonejs.org

[26] http://www.adamretter.org.uk/papers/restful-xquery_january-2012.pdf

[27] http://id.loc.gov/authorities/names.html

[28] http://viaf.org/

[29] http://worldcat.org/identities/

[30] Reviews were selected for transcription by author, rather than by work, so some reception items discuss works that are not themselves published in WWO, though other works by that author are.

[31] For the WWP, at least, given the project's long-term approach to research and publication.

Author's keywords for this paper: metadata; XML; JSON; TEI; XQuery; XSLT; web applications

Ashley M. Clark

Ashley M. Clark serves as the XML Applications Developer for the Northeastern University Libraries' Digital Scholarship Group (DSG). She works on TAPAS and the Women Writers Project, specializing in XML databases, XQuery, and XSLT.

Sarah Connell

Sarah Connell is the Project Manager for the Women Writers Project and a member of the Digital Scholarship Group at Northeastern University. Her current research explores applications of literary theory through text encoding, working with early modern national histories.

Balisage Series on Markup Technologies

Link to the Balisage Proceedings Home Page at http://www.balisage.net/Proceedings
Link to this paper (entry page with links) at http://www.balisage.net/Proceedings/vol18/html/Feldman01/BalisageVol18-Feldman01.html

XML In, Web Out: International Symposium on sub rosa XML

Proceedings

Message Format Persistence in Large Enterprise Systems

Damon Feldman
Solutions Director
MarkLogic Corporation

XML In, Web Out: International Symposium on sub rosa XML
August 1, 2016

Copyright © 2016 by the author. Used with permission.

How to cite this paper

Feldman, Damon. "Message Format Persistence in Large Enterprise Systems." Presented at XML In, Web Out: International Symposium on sub rosa XML, Washington, DC, August 1, 2016. In *Proceedings of XML In, Web Out: International Symposium on sub rosa XML*. Balisage Series on Markup Technologies, vol. 18 (2016). DOI: 10.4242/BalisageVol18.Feldman01.

Abstract

It is more efficient to store messages as-is or with minimal modification than it is to develop a new (typically relational) schema to re-map and store the data in the messages. Yet, persistent models and message models have different needs, so naïve message persistence may not be ideal. We review the approach used in two enterprise integration efforts where XML message formats are directly or nearly-directly used to persist data and enable functions in the enterprise, avoiding costly and fragile mapping layers and the associated impedance mismatch.

We also make the general case that the message model is more critical to enterprise architecture (as distinct from system architecture) and should therefore be preeminent during enterprise design.

Actual integration efforts on the HealthCare.gov Data Services Hub and a large insurance provider are discussed, and simplified, non-proprietary example documents are used to illustrate the concepts concretely. We also review and define the Data Hub pattern for integrating data in the service of real-time, transactional loads that support service oriented communication across systems via messages.

The architectural implications of sharing message and persistent document structures, rather than using a separate persistence model, is far-reaching and affects multiple layers or "tiers" in the overall architecture. The extent of this change illustrates that NoSQL technology, which can store message-like persistent forms, drives a fundamentally different architectural approach rather than merely being another persistence option.

Table of Contents

Messages are preeminent in enterprise architecture
Alternate approaches to Message Modeling
    Focus on cardinality

Readability and intelligibility
Beware conventional modeling tools
Persisting document and message models
HealthCare.gov Data Services Hub
Processing
How DSH stores message data directly
Message format persistence
Additional data
Rapid application development and flexibility
Direct search and query of the persisted message model
Agility
Storing data "as-is"
DSH as enterprise integration using a message model
Large, Commercial Insurance Provider
What is a Data Hub?
High-level architecture
Core business objects used in message formats
Common Messaging Formats
Flexible messages - but canonical persistent forms
Data chunks as building blocks
Database optimization
Data Chunking for re-use
Data Chunks vs Basic Types
Data Chunks as dynamic message construction
Common Message Models
Architecture implications
Message Models as Primary Drivers of Architecture
Efficiencies from persisting message model components
Summary
NoSQL technology alters the overall architecture

Messages are preeminent in enterprise architecture

We assert here that defining message formats (typically XML and JSON in today's systems) are the most critical design decision of enterprise integration, and this emphasis puts the overall enterprise architecture in tension with the needs of individual (sub-) system design, where other concerns are paramount.

Consider the following diagram of three systems being integrated.

Figure 1

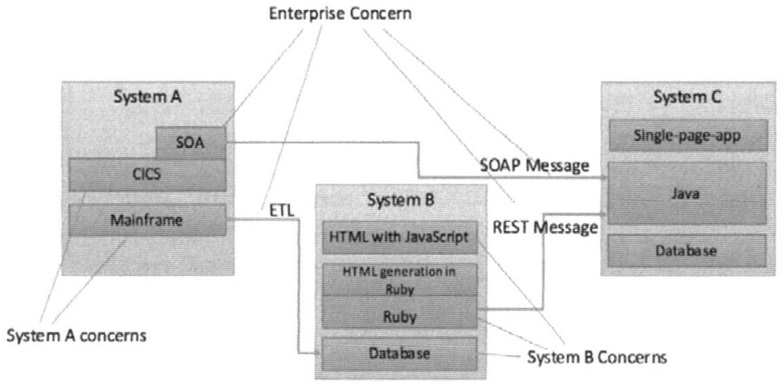

Multiple systems integrated by Messages. Each system has internal architectural concerns separate from the overall enterprise architectural concerns.

Each system individually has its own design and concerns, ranging from relational schema design, to a good modular organization of the CICS code, to having a good object model for the Ruby or Java tiers. The overall enterprise (the resulting system of systems depicted by the entire diagram) however, is substantially unaffected by these per-system concerns, as each system is or should be a black box accessible only through APIs that are built around Message Formats. Therefore, Message Formats and the model they are based on are far more of an enterprise concern, as distinct from individual systems concerns, and in fact, enterprise and system design may be in conflict.

Given that enterprise and per-system concerns will sometimes be in conflict, which should be privileged? In a larger enterprise, the Message Model is more difficult to change and has a broader impact, as it is used by many or even all systems to communicate. The software re-work involved in changing many systems may be prohibitive in itself, and the cross-team coordination needed to change many systems at once is far more prohibitive than the software work itself.

In fact, one expects most individual systems to be replaced over time. Clean integration via well-defined messages (APIs) eases the task of replacing these individual (sub-) systems. In essence, Message Formats and the APIs built on them enable and impose a componentization on the total enterprise with clean interfaces among them. This feature of an Enterprise cannot be overstated, as the ability to divide large, complex tasks into manageable components is a fundamental tenant of computer science .

The domain model representing core business entities within the API messages, in contrast, is difficult to change, shared across multiple systems and involved most directly in enterprise-wide integration between the component sub-systems.

The preceding aspects of Message Models, their role in enterprise architectures and their larger importance relative to individual system concerns all suggest that architects start with Message Models, and then adapt our systems to use them effectively rather than the converse.

This then leads to the techniques in this paper – how to focus first and primarily on enterprise models for communication, and then use the resulting Message Models as the persistent model, or store a persistent model as close to it as possible.

In particular, this makes document modeling more important, and suggests that our document modeling practices and tools should be used for enterprise architecture, rather than legacy tools.

Alternate approaches to Message Modeling

Unfortunately, much of our enterprise modeling is focused on entity-relational modeling and related logical models, which are closely tied to relational modeling practices, or is focused on UML modeling which arises from object oriented modeling.

Logical Models are a work around that can address this mismatch to some extent, forming the basis of a Message Model with reduced baggage from E-R or OOP modeling, but logical modeling practices are still grounded in the other technologies they spring from, including use of E-R and OOP tools, an (arguable) over-emphasis on cardinalities (which drive relational models but not message models) and other baggage.

Below are two subtle ways in which current modeling practices privilege and focus implicitly on relational models, to the detriment of the more important document models.

Focus on cardinality

Typical enterprise models focus on cardinality. In markup such as XML and JSON, as well as in RDF, cardinality is not typically important. XML representing someone with one address may look like this:

```
<person>
   <name>bob jones</name>
   <address> 123 Wall St, New York, NY </address>
<person>
```

and a relational model can also represent the same data:

Table I

PERSON_ID	NAME	ADDRESS
5538	bob jones	123 Wall St, New York, NY

The XML model is easily amended to hold an arbitrary number of addresses:

```
<person>
   <name>bob jones</name>
   <address> 123 Wall St, New York, NY</address>
   <address> 76 Seaside Terrace, The Hamptons, NY</address>
<person>
```

Where in a relational model, changing cardinalities from 1:1 to 1:N requires additional tables and a join key to be in third normal form.

Table II

PERSON_ID	NAME
5538	bob jones

Table III

ADDRESS_ID	PERSON_ID_FK	ADDRESS
22	5538	123 Wall St, New York, NY
23	5538	76 Seaside Terrace, The Hamptons, NY

Clearly, cardinality is of critical importance to relational modeling as getting that wrong requires a disruptive change, and cardinality drives third normal form modeling, E-R diagramming and related practices. In contrast, cardinality is less important for XML or JSON message modeling.

Other modeling approaches such as UML are similarly infected with a concern for cardinality, as cardinality determines the data structure (Array vs. single value) needed in object-oriented code, so it must be called out on models that drive functions, classes and method implementation.

Readability and intelligibility

Documents are human readable, where E-R diagrams and related models are machine readable. This is because of hierarchy and the need to follow pointers or links.

The evidence for this is informal but compelling. Documents emerged organically from human societies – insurance applications, messages, contracts, bills of material, articles and books (including this one) have been organized hierarchically for centuries, and such organization suits the human mind well.

Pointers and tables, however, are confusing and difficult to follow for a human. One must often literally follow the lines on a complex E-R diagram to understand what is related to what. Many readers of this paper will recall the experience of walking up to a huge E-R diagram on plotter paper or taped together from many smaller sheets and attempting to trace the various connections to the tables and entities in an attempt to understand what is related to what.

Often, the maintainer of the diagram will try (with limited success) to group related tables into particular areas of the diagram, thus imposing one level of hierarchical organization on a spaghetti bowl diagram of inter-connected tables or entities. This minimal hierarchy is helpful, but illustrates that the fundamental approach is suited to relational modeling or object-oriented programming rather than document modeling.

Beware conventional modeling tools

We include this discussion here to suggest that we, as an industry, need to re-examination our typical modeling practices, and that document modeling should be elevated as the primary goal of modeling in a large enterprise, tools such as schema editors, UML, or new approaches should be considered that ease the development of document models, and each practitioner should be clear if they are building a "good model" informed by decades of relational modeling, or a "good model" based on how the document model and derived Message Models will function.

Persisting document and message models

The above is to make the case that document models should be considered first and with increased priority in a moderate sized or large enterprise, that tooling should primarily be evaluated by its ability to support document models, that architects should consider document models primarily as they create data models.

But what about the relational and other models? Creating a model that works for both relational and message models is difficult and requires extensive transforms to implement. Object models further complicate the situation, but as graphs they are more similar to documents (which are trees) so here we confine ourselves to the issue of having relational and message models coexist.

Below, we describe two enterprises that were simplified and improved by focusing first on the message models, and then using those same message models as a persistent model to the extent practical. Specific issues and techniques are listed that helped make this approach work well.

HealthCare.gov Data Services Hub

In the HealthCare.gov Data Services Hub (DSH), all message traffic flowing into, out of, and through the hub is (almost-) directly stored to enable traceability and other business functions for the overall system. The data in message payloads is modified prior to storage only to the extent needed to de-identify personal information, drop irrelevant data and add standardized metadata such as timestamps, message type and uniform success/error codes. This was implemented using NoSQL transform and storage, so the persistence was achieved with minimal additional data modeling or schema development – only the additional metadata and decisions of what to redact was modeled – and the overall effort was simple and rapid to develop.

As always, the key was that the data was already modeled (in the message model) so there was substantial benefit in not re-modeling the bulk of the data, and only modeling differences.

For context, HealthCare.gov has three major components. The first component is the Federally Facilitated Marketplace (FFM) which is the web site that consumers interact with to apply for and choose insurance plans. Second is the Data Services Hub (DSH) which is a message service that proxies and coordinates requests to various government and private entities, providing a clean, uniform API to the FFM and state exchanges, while hiding the complexities of communication with myriad other systems. The third is the MIDAS data warehouse, which performs analytics and other downstream processing.

Figure 2

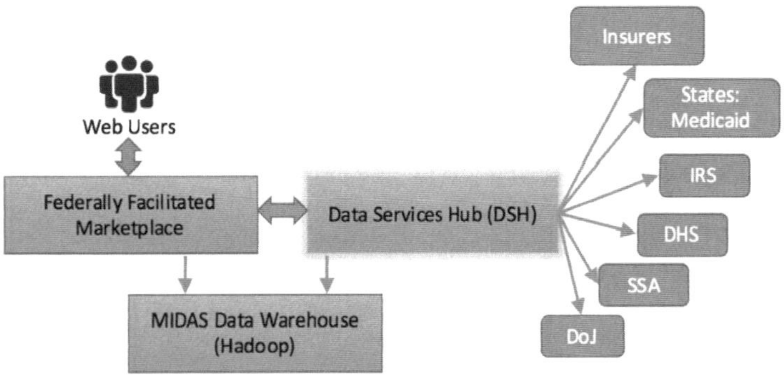

Overall Affordable Care Act systems, showing DSH which provides consistent messaging to the overall enterprise

Numerous articles have been written about the lack of monitoring, infrastructure issues, and general rockiness of the overall HealthCare.gov launch (https://www.advisory.com/daily-briefing/2014/03/03/time-inside-the-nightmare-launch-of-healthcaregov), but less well known is the success of the Data Services Hub component, which was developed under the same tight time constraints as FFM. DSH integrates services from the Internal Revenue Service, Department of Homeland Security, Social Security Administration, Department of Justice, Peace Corps, Office of Personnel Management, as well as many insurance providers. These data sources are used to verify income, check prison status, validate social security numbers and other tasks. Some of the data sources are stored as copies of US Federal Government data within the DSH system, but most are accessed in real time from source systems outside DSH, through APIs hosted by the data-owning government agency.

Processing

The process of calling the DSH and processing a request is conceived of as having four "legs."

- The first leg is an incoming web service request to DSH containing an XML body.
- The second leg is a request to an authoritative data source – typically a REST endpoint using XML payloads – hosted by an external Federal agency.
- The third leg is the response from that authoritative data source.
- Finally, the fourth leg is the return of an XML service response to the caller.

As one may imagine, there are other complexities such as multi-step processes where a message is split into many sub-requests which are combined using internal workflow and state persistence, deferred due to outage windows, routed to a multi-day, human-in-the-loop review processes, translated to REST, X12 or other formats and the like, but these four legs constitute the essential workflow of every call in the system.

How DSH stores message data directly

As noted above, messages flowing through DSH are stored with minimal modification as persistent data. Each of these four legs transmits and processes different data, but all are XML message formats and all a record of all messages for all legs are stored by the DSH.

If this data were stored, say, in relational form, a complex XML to relational mapping process would be needed for each and every message. Some designers would even introduce a third model – an object oriented model – in a Java tier in between the messages and relational persistence to parse the XML to POJOs only to then transform the data to tabular.

This additional mapping and modeling would have been cost and time prohibitive because of the modeling, the mapping, and the overhead and delay needed for every message or API change. Any change to an API or message format would require a new relational model, new mappings, new DDL to provision the model, and upgrade scripts and coordination to change existing data if the system was already in production.

Instead, saving the message with minimal modification has proven to be efficient and powerful. The business benefits include: enabling historic auditing and data lineage, monitoring the system for issues in real time, support of forensic investigations into data or system problems, and helping correct any consumer issues that may be found.

The portion of DSH that stores message traffic in this manner was designed and implemented in the final few months of the DSH development. The component of DSH is called the Event Management Framework, from the notion that receiving, processing and sending events are "events" within the DSH system. The bulk of system development prior to this feature also used documents as the primary persistent mechanism (for state management, workflow and other functions) but is beyond the scope of this paper.

Message format persistence

As described above, the persistent format leveraged and closely resembled the message model, and a NoSQL storage product was used that natively stores and transforms XML. The benefit was to use as much of the message model as possible, specifying only differences – how was this accomplished?

The design goal was to use existing structures to the extent possible, and specify only additional data and removed data relative to the message model. This is somewhat in the spirit of object-oriented modeling, where the differences between a subclass and superclass are specified in the subclass, and common structure and functionality is "inherited."

Additional data

Additional data was added by creating a wrapper schema to capture key metadata such as message type, success vs. error result, timestamp and other metadata. The actual message payloads are not re-modeled for persistence and the schema allows for the full (or partial) message to be stored as an xs:any with only these minimal tracking and reporting fields added. For this reason, the schema is considered a wrapper schema where very little data is specified and the bulk of the data is whatever message was flowing through the system (subject to a de-identification transform).

```
<message-event xmlns="http://cms.gov/dsh/EMF">
  <metadata>
    <timestamp>2013-10-02T18:22:33.444</timestamp>
    <service>minimal insurance coverage confirmation</service>
    <success>successful</success>
        <stateOrTerritory>Texas</stateOrTerritory>
  </metadata>
  <result>
    <opm:insuranceCheck xmlns:opm="http://opm.gov/insure>
      <opm:insuranceExists>true</opm:insuranceExists>
      <opm:typecode>44b</opm:typecode>
      <opm:ssn>REDACT FOR DSH<opm:ssn>
      <opm:insuredStartDate>
      [. . .]
```


Instead of xs:any, one could us the message schema as the payload inside of the <result> element. However, one would then need to manage one wrapper schema per message type and update it whenever a message format or service API changes.

Note that the message-event, timestamp, success flag, and <result> element are in the "http://cms.gov /dsh/EMF" namespace as they are defined by DSH and used for internal storage, but the child element of <result> is a (notional) OPM message describing whether someone is already insured via a federal program. The messages from external services are typically much larger than the minimal metadata elements defined by DSH, so the bulk of the persistent format is being used as-is.

The example shows the <opm:ssn> element as "REDACTED." In reality, personally identifiable information (PII) elements that pose a privacy risk are completely removed at DSH, but it is shown as redacted in this synthetic document for clarity. The de-identification process was implemented because, per policy, the DSH cannot store personally identifiable information, personal health information, or federal tax information (PII, PHI or FTI).

The message uses the powerful "envelope pattern" where some raw or useful data is stored separately from additional data or metadata. Here the additional data is message metadata and is in the <metadata> element at the top of the document.

Rapid application development and flexibility

A "dashboard" capability was developed within the DSH atop this model to aggregate and filter system activity based on event types, destinations, times, success and error codes, and other information (primarily the <metadata> information illustrated above). These dashboards can answer questions such as: how many enrollment request to Kaiser Health were rejected (based on metadata holding error codes) for the state of Texas during the disk failover period from 1:15am to 1:37am on December 17th? Were they retried?

Direct search and query of the persisted message model

Text search is enabled on the entire record inside the <result> section, which is particularly useful when an ID is available. IDs may be shared across disparate messages, but tend to be unique allowing an analyst to quickly narrow down all traffic for a particular identifier. Certain readable codes or descriptions in messages may also be searched as text.

XQuery and XPath can also be used to search the stored data by building queries and path expressions that access one specific message format, such as a certain IRS response format used for income verification.

The NoSQL product used supported text and XQuery on XML without additional systems integration, making this appealing.

Agility

New message formats were simple to add to the system. The developers merely wrapped any new SOAP or REST request to be captured with the metadata elements above, wrote a de-identification XSLT transform, and sent the resulting structure (now with metadata and without PII) to a tracing endpoint. While DSH applied this de-identifying transform to filter out PII to comply with specific DSH regulations, another project using this approach would likely store the entire record as a child of the <result> element.

As very little data is considered PII, PHI or FTI, the de-identification transforms were simple (names, social security numbers, addresses and the like) and were based on a known list of elements that may represent PII or other sensitive data.

This might be done as follows

```
<xsl:stylesheet version="2.0" xmlns:xsl="http://www.w3.org/1999/XSL/Transform">

 <xsl:param
    name="removeElementsNamed"
    select="'givenName|familyName|ssn|phone|addressLine1'"/>

 <xsl:template match="node()|@*" name="identity">
  <xsl:copy>
   <xsl:apply-templates select="node()|@*"/>
  </xsl:copy>
 </xsl:template>

 <xsl:template match=
 "*[name() = tokenize($removeElementsNamed, '\|')]"/>
</xsl:stylesheet>
```

where the select attribute holds a list of XML local-names of elements to redact.

This is a "blacklist" approach, where the elements to be removed are explicitly listed either in code or some configuration file. A "whitelist" approach is also possible, where only fields known to not be sensitive are retained. A whitelist approach is more complex, slower, and requires at least some comprehensive examination of all schemas involved. For those reasons, specific removal of known "blacklisted" elements was chosen for DSH.

The DSH use of messages illustrates how modeling, translation and code are reduced by re-using message data directly as a persistent format, and storing data in a form that is as close to the message format as possible.

Storing data "as-is"

Because the message formats did (and as agued above, should) exist prior to the persistence need, we can call this storing data "as-is" which emphasizes the benefit of aligning message and persistent models and storing documents.

DSH as enterprise integration using a message model

Conceptually, a portion of the US Federal Government spanning multiple agencies is functioning as a single enterprise by virtue of their integration with the DSH. Messages built on a uniform data model integrate all these systems, with the primary data consumer being the Department of Health and Human Services' HealthCare.gov program.

This is therefore architecturally an Enterprise Integration effort based on design and use of a coherent message model, despite the systems involved being maintained and operated by different Federal and state agencies as well as private companies.

This is a version of enterprise integration where existing systems are integrated by a new model, but not an example of a system where a new model is pushed down by governance to existing systems, to be used internally across the enterprise. That is, the overall enterprise is integrated by a common message model, and the new analytics/tracking component then leveraged this message model for persistence. However legacy and externally-managed systems continued to use their own internal object and persistence models, and in fact continued to use their own message models, which were converted to a common model within DSH.

We now turn to an example where the message model is built a priori and used more extensively to support interoperability across the enterprise.

Large, Commercial Insurance Provider

A large insurance provider also built a system that stores message formats with minimal modification. This system uses a "Data Hub" architectural pattern where data from many disparate systems are stored and integrated data into a consolidated Data Hub. This Data Hub then provides actionable, real-time information and services across the enterprise.

What is a Data Hub?

A Data Hub is a centralized persistent store that gathers data from numerous (disparate) systems of record or data silos, on a periodic basis or in real-time, and stores all data in one place and one form.

The Data Hub then becomes the preferred source for various kinds of data, and likely the only source for integrated, cross-line-of-business data. The Data Hub becomes the ideal place to access data due to its scalability, convenience and de-coupling from transactional systems, and upstream transactional systems typically remain the systems of record and handle new data capture, workflow, and end-user interactions.

Note that the prior example was the CMS "Data Services Hub" which is a specific computer system that loosely conforms to the Data Hub pattern; but here we have an insurance provider using a more generic "Data Hub" architectural pattern to build a central repository. The insurance provider Data Hub stores but the core business data for the insurer using message formats for efficiency (both computational and software delivery efficiency). In contrast the DSH stored a record of messages flowing into and through the DSH for analytics and monitoring.

The primary difference is that the DSH is for downstream analysis and forensics, where this Data Hub implementation provides real-time APIs that expose consolidated data to the rest of the enterprise to support service-oriented architecture (SOA) patterns and transactional workloads. This real-time, transactional support of a SOA is in contrast to a Data Lake or Data Warehouse which are typically analytic, and cannot support real-time,, transactional loads.

High-level architecture

Figure 3

Data Hub interaction with systems of record, systems of interaction, and one MDM system

The diagram above illustrates the insurance company's Data Hub enterprise ecosystem, including four systems of record – one for Providers (doctors, pharmacists, dentists and labs), two for claims processing, and one for membership. In addition to these systems of record, it also includes a legacy Master Data Management (MDM) system that manages the merging and splitting of identities, and two interaction systems that consume data but do not store much of their own data. The interaction systems need access to consolidated data to provide accurate, up-to-date information, and the systems of record also have a (lesser) need for enterprise data. For example, the membership system may need to evaluate a member's risk or claims history by accessing a member's consolidated claims history.

This pattern allows for both operational isolation and increased functionality in the Data Hub. E.g. the Doctor Finder application includes geospatial and text searching, where the providers system of record does not. Some of the systems of record did not support online transaction loads that are supported by the more robust Data Hub infrastructure and software.

Not shown are bulk exports to a downstream analytic Data Lake based on Hadoop that performs most reporting and analytic functions. Since the data is exported to the Data Hub and the data hub has larger processing capacity than the systems of record, the Data Hub then exports data to the Data Lake without incurring an additional bulk read from the various systems of record.

Data Hubs are distinguished from ESBs and virtual databases in that they store data and index it in one place, rather than coordinating many queries and transforms in real time, provide unique indexing and analytics, and allow operational separation from source systems via separate disks and servers.

Core business objects used in message formats

The insurer's Data Hub provides services using a consistent message format within well-defined APIs to the entire the enterprise. These messages may combine data from multiple data domains (such as membership, claims and payment). The messages have simple request/response headers wrapping a core Business Entity model, which is coherently designed – meaning naming conventions and overall style are consistent across all business entities, regardless of the services or business domain for a particular message.

Here is a notional response message which we see has some elements near the top that are generic to all requests returning lists of items (<total-results>, <page> and <page-size>), and the <result-item> element then holds a Business Entity or list of Entities – in this case medical claims.

```
<claim-history-response xmlns="http://insurer.com/response">
  <total-results>240</total-results>
  <page>1</page>
  <page-size>20</page-size>
  <result-list>
    <result-item>
      <claim:medical-claim xmlns:claim="http://insurer.com/claims">
        <patient-id>124799819</patient-id>
        <claim-date>2015-02-02</claim-date>
        <primary-problem code="icd-9">250.01</primary-problem>
        <provider-id>9981772</provider-id>
        <claim-line>
          <procedure>
            <code system=HCPCS”>J1815</code>
            <description>insulin injection per 5 units</description>
          </procedure>
          <claim-amount unit=”USD”>253.28</claim-amount>
        </claim-line>
      </claim>
    </result-item>
  </result-list>
</claim-history-response>
```

Physically, this Data Hub runs on a clustered, distributed database, is easier to scale up with massively-parallel or elastic infrastructure, has less frequent and more predictable outage windows, is fully highly-available (HA) and has other advantages as a system explicitly built for this kind of high-volume, consolidated data access.

As with the HealthCare.gov DSH, the insurer Data Hub runs on an enterprise-class NoSQL distributed database comprising multiple primary nodes and a similar number of standby nodes at a remote disaster recovery site, synchronized by database replication. This level of disaster recovery and clustering are not available for all the upstream, transactional systems, making the Data Hub more robust and available and also more easy to administer than a federation of the disparate upstream products and systems.

Common Messaging Formats

To provide common services using common messaging formats, the insurer's Data Hub implementation also stores data in the messaging formats themselves. The above data structure has a clear delineation between message management data (in the http://insurer.com/response namespace) and business data (in per-domain namespaces such as http://insurer.com/claims).

However, there are two minor changes to the overall messaging format used to persist it, with specific motivations for each.

Flexible messages - but canonical persistent forms

First, persistent document formats must, curiously, be less flexible than message document formats. Messages vary from caller to caller and service to service, but the persistent format must be uniform across all instances to be easily queried. Therefore, the Data Hub had to choose and specify one particular form of the messaging format for persistence.

The example above returns a list of claims at a summary level, but others will return a complete insurance claim together with associated data about the provider giving care and the member filing the claim (that is: non-claim membership and provider data from another data domain).

To achieve this aim, the Data Hub stores data in one, predictable format, but serves it in many formats, requiring the persistent model to be transformed and re-packaged when needed to satisfy various services and APIs. The primary difference among the different message formats is one of what we will call "data extent" – how many related elements are packaged together into one document. Therefore the data modeling challenge is to support re-packaging of re-usable data building blocks.

Here is an example persistent document showing the larger persistent data extent which includes another data chunk beyond that which is in the claim message above.

```
<claim:medical-claim xmlns:claim="http://insurer.com/claims">
<patient-id>124799819</patient-id>
<claim-date>2015-02-02</claim-date>
<primary-problem code="icd-9">250.01</primary-problem>
<provider-id>9981772</provider-id>
<payments>
    <claim-payment>
        <paid-date>2015-03-05</paid-date>
        <payee>
            <payee-type>group practice</payee-type>
            <payee-name>Yakenflaster Health Group</payee-name>
            <payee-id>787877211</payee-id>
        </payee>
    </claim-payment>
</payments>
<claim-line>
    <procedure>
        <code system=HCPCS">J1815</code>
            <description>insulin injection per 5 units</description>
    </procedure>
    <claim-amount unit="USD">253.28</claim-amount>
</claim-line>
</claim>
```

This persistent document differs from the above message form in that the message header data about pagination and similar is not present, there is one claim per document rather than many, and that in the <claim> business entity there is an additional <claim-payment> data chunk which is not in the message. (This notional XML document is substantially simpler than the actual data to allow it to be easily shown here.)

Data chunks as building blocks

Rather than have arbitrary additions, re-groupings and transformations when building messages from the persistent documents, the data model identifies such "data chunks" which are preferentially deleted, added or re-combined. In the example above the <claim-payment> element and its child elements are an information a "chunk" so it was in keeping with the design philosophy to remove it as a unit when determining the message format from the persistent format. Removing a completely arbitrary set of elements or running an arbitrary data transform is possible and used in some instances, but avoided in favor of adding or removing at the chunk level where possible.

These data chunks are therefore the units of use and re-use in the data model, particularly as the message model is re-used to construct the persistent model.

The Data Chunk approach seen in the above example is covered in more detail below.

Database optimization

The second change from the message format to the persistent document format is the addition of database-specific information such as ingest dates, data lineage (traceability to original source system), join keys, RDF data added to support automated reasoning and semantic integration, and the like.

This addition of internal data is similar to the DSH addition of message metadata, and is also accomplished using the envelope pattern.

The added internal data is typically used to optimize queries and support database functions, auditing, data quality and governance and is not used in the message formats. When the persistent document is converted to a message, this additional data is dropped.

Here is a notional persistent document that also includes database-specific information in a <header> element:

```
<envelope>
    <header xmlns="http://insurance.com/db-header">
        <identifiers>
            <id>9981772</id>
            <id>787877211</id>
        </identifiers>
        <snomed-codes>
            <code src="250.1">44054006</code>
            <code src="HCPCS">237599002</code>
        </snomed-codes>
        <triples> ... RDF data here ... </triples>
    </header>
    <business-entity>
        <claim:medical-claim xmlns:claim="http://insurer.com/claims">
            <patient-id>124799819</patient-id>
            <claim-date>2015-02-02</claim-date>
            <primary-problem code="icd-9">250.01</primary-problem>
            <provider-id>9981772</provider-id>
            <payments>
                <claim-payment>
                    <paid-date>2015-03-05</paid-date>
                    <payee>
                        <payee-type>group practice</payee-type>
                        <payee-name>Yakenflaster Health Group</payee-name>
                        <payee-id>787877211</payee-id>
                    </payee>
                </claim-payment>
            </payments>
            <claim-line>
                <procedure>
                    <code system=HCPCS”>J1815</code>
                        <description>insulin injection per 5 units</description>
                </procedure>
                <claim-amount unit=”USD”>253.28</claim-amount>
            </claim-line>
            </claim>
    </business-entity>
</envelope>
```

In this persistent message both changes are shown – the additional data chunk of <payments> that was excluded from the message form, and the <header> element with the following internal database information:

- A list of IDs. These were added in this system to provide a guaranteed numeric form despite some IDs being alphanumeric, which allows faster numeric key joins between records when querying the Data Hub.
- A set of related medical concepts coded in SNOMED terminology. This is notional for simplicity. The ICD9 and HCPCS systems have incompatible codes, so to provide semantic interoperability and simple querying, it is useful to convert all medical concepts into one terminology set.
- Semantic triples (typically in RDF format). The particular NoSQL product used combines document storage with RDF storage, and supports SPARQL queries over the claim data to the extent that some information is stored in the header as triples.

Data Chunking for re-use

The data chunk approach provided substantial, but not completely arbitrary, flexibility in building different data extents. E.g. for the insurance company, the data chunks can be re-combined to support both a small Claim Summary message and also a larger, detailed Claim description message.

Data Chunks vs Basic Types

Determining the size of a data chunk is a key design choice. In Chessell15 atomic, re-usable entities are called "Basic Types." Basic Types, in Chessell, et al, are exactly the un-changed smaller pieces of information that do not change from place to place in the model. They may be addresses, effective date ranges, telephone contact information and the like.

However, when substantively re-using a Message Model throughout the technology stack and persisting it (nearly) as-is, much larger chunks can be re-used and standardized than envisioned by Chessell et al. This is because in traditional systems, the models must be radically re-modeled (because traditional systems use a relational persistent model, a hierarchical XML messaging model and a graph-shaped Object Model – all of which are incompatible to some extent). The Data Hub approach uses the same fundamental model – a hierarchical document model – at all layers, therefore re-use can be far higher, with hierarchy being preserved across layers.

Re-use of the preeminent or pre-existing Message Model allows the chunk size and granularity of re-use to be much larger. Certainly tens or hundreds of data fields is acceptable in many cases for a chunk, rather than only a few. For the insurer, Data Chunks represented a "core" claim with vital claim information together with additional data chunks for conceptually separate claim processing information, claim lines, provider information, historic information, claim review information and so on.

This diagram illustrates that the persistent model data chunks are recombined to form different message formats, allowing re-use at the chunk level, but also flexibility in message formats.

Figure 4

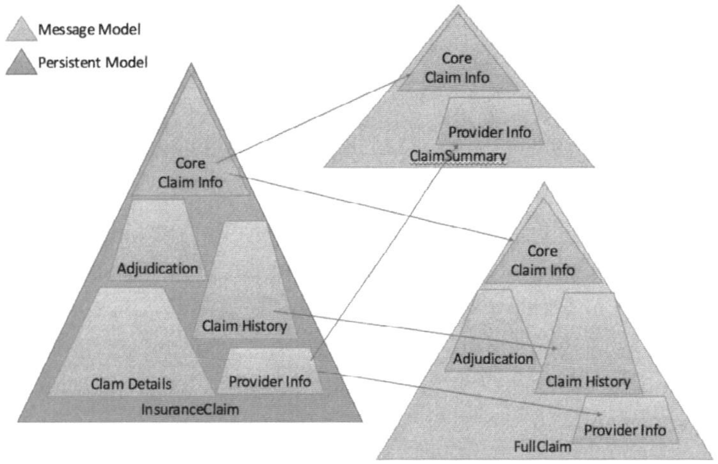

This diagram illustrates that the persistent model data chunks are recombined to form different message formats, allowing re-use at the chunk level, but also flexibility in message formats.

These chunks are not the persistent documents, but rather are the building blocks of both persistent and message documents (the insurer used XML, so the messages and persisted entities were "documents." If JSON were used they would be called objects or entities). This insurer was using XML Schema for modeling, so the chunks were defined as types and various master schemas imported these types to include them in the overall schemas.

Ideally, many messages will correspond exactly to the persistent form, with no additional chunks added, or extraneous chunks removed. That is, the persistent form should be chosen to include a set of chunks that is the most natural and commonly served message form. This way, message formation at runtime is as fast and simple as possible, and coding of transforms is minimized.

This is easiest when there is one well-known and expected Message format – e.g. healthcare systems use HL7 CCD documents to transmit patient summaries. Other message formats will require some re-combination of the chunks and will incur at least minimal performance overhead, though still far less than a wholesale transformation from relational to message formats, or even field-by-field transformation between disparate document formats.

Data Chunks as dynamic message construction

One typical form of combination is to create summary records, such as a Member summaries. The Member summary may contain some Member data chunks, and also have non-member data such as payment and recent claim activity. This cross-domain message is intuitively not ideal for persistence because it crosses domains and is very particular to a summarization use case.

By gathering the chunks of related entities into a summary message, the system is effectively summarizing and providing related information (e.g. last 20 claims) with core information (e.g. basic member information).

Relationships among data chunks can be represented with RDF (semantic triples) or other graph technologies. Documents + graphs combine to form a powerful data representation approach as documents represent trees well (but not graphs) and graphs model relationships naturally (but don't highlight natural hierarchies as found in trees).

This approach is actually quite similar to Dynamic Semantic Publishing (DSP -such as implemented at the BBC and described in Rayfield12 http://www.bbc.co.uk/blogs/bbcinternet/2012/04/sports_dynamic_semantic.html) where documents are statically stored as XML or HTML and then dynamically assembled based on semantic rules and ontologies. Here we are dynamically "publishing" the message format needed rather than an article, e-book or web page. While a detailed analysis of similarities between dynamic message construction and DSP are beyond the scope of this paper, note that the DSP approach often uses RDF and ontologies to assemble information as needed.

Common Message Models

Both the HealthCare.gov DSH and the insurer rely on a common message model. The model was the single Message Model for DSH, and was the set of flexible Message Formats built from reusable data chunks for the insurer.

As with many things in computer science, such a hub-and-spoke model is needed to simplify communications among many components. The number of translations needed to implement point-to-point communications among N components is famously N(N-1)/2, but the number of translations needed to implement a hub/spoke model is N. Therefore, common message models simplify enterprise integration.

Using the common message model as a persistent format continues and extends the cost savings and agility of the common model. It is enabled by the rise of non-relational (aka NoSQL) databases and data management techniques which can directly accept either XML or JSON data, store it, index it, and query it.

Architecture implications

Using data chunks as the building blocks of documents provides re-use between the persistent model and the message models in an enterprise. Only the differences need be additionally modeled once the enterprise message model is complete.

To summarize how differences are specified in examples above, these differences include:

- Message metadata added to DSH persistent documents, such as dates, types and success codes
- PII removal from DSH messages before persistence per policy
- Message header addition to messages in the Insurance Provider data hub
- Data chunk repackaging, combining, and removal in the insurer Data Hub
- Database-only fields for optimizations, auditing and data governance in the insurer Data Hub

The key advantage being that the actual domain models comprising all business data did not need to be re-modeled or mapped in either system.

This architecture allowed development efficiencies where an additional model was not created, and computational efficiencies where messages in the Insurance Provider case were largely de-normalized and ready to serve via APIs and services.

This is a substantial conceptual shift from the traditional approach. Typically, and for decades, message models have been XML, JSON, EDI or similar, and persisted data has been relational as defined by an entity-relation (E-R) model. Often an object model is added to the mix (as though someone thought that when two models are good, three must be better). These models are all fundamentally incompatible and enterprise modeling techniques (such as Model-driven Architecture and logical modeling) formed to ease the mapping and impedance mismatch problems inherent in the formerly-ubiquitous underlying technologies.

In the DSH and insurance provider systems described above, where message models drive the architecture the goal was no longer to work around the model incompatibilities, but rather to manage the re-packaging and chunking of re-usable data. Arguably, this focus is more critical to the business and directly calls out areas of commonality and re-use, rather than having architecture and data modeling focused on remediating mapping problems.

Message Models as Primary Drivers of Architecture

Both the DSH and insurer systems were large systems-of-systems, where pre-existing, independent systems were being pulled together into an enterprise-wide whole. For DSH, that whole spanned HealthCare.gov and multiple involved US Federal Government systems. For the insurance provider, the whole spanned various Membership, Claim, Identity, Provider (doctor) systems, and other COTS or legacy products.

Each sub-system may have its own internal data formats, separate from the common enterprise message model. It may have its own relational schema, separate from other components schema and from the common formats used across the enterprise. These become implementation details that are irrelevant to the way the sub-systems participate in the overall enterprise. The overall enterprise is connected and made to function as a whole using a common message model and the APIs that include those messages. This is perhaps the core idea behind a service-oriented architecture for enterprise integration.

This integration approach is useful in all contexts, but is particularly enabled by direct persistence of XML, JSON or other message formats to make the entire enterprise more agile and efficient, in addition to being integrated.

Efficiencies from persisting message model components

The efficiency and agility of persisting message data comes from the two shifts implicit in the approaches described above.

First, there is no need to re-model the bulk of the data. Since integration is the primary concern in combining a number of systems into a coherent enterprise, the message formats can come first. The advantages of a hub-and-spoke approach dictate that a single common model is developed (modulo data chunks where different messages include more or less data as composed of different data chunks). Avoiding re-modeling the data is a large savings vis the typical approach, and also speeds up application development, mitigates risk and reduces complexity.

Second, the insurer's approach, in particular, allows architecture to re-focus on the concerns of identifying re-usable data chunks and packaging and re-packaging them into a variety of messages. This packaging and re-packaging is more fundamental to the business than simple translations among incompatible formats, and is amenable to semantic technology that describes links and collections among chunks.

Summary

Two major initiatives are described above where a message model was developed first, to provide an efficient hub-and-spoke integration among disparate systems or data silos.

In both cases, these messages are a key element of overall enterprise integration, whereby data from many sub-systems are made available across lines of business and enterprise silos. In addition, "sub-rosa" (under the table), these same interchange formats are persisted with minimal changes and repackaging, in these two cases as XML using NoSQL persistent stores that process XML and JSON natively.

Agility was achieved by the insurer by re-using their core messaging model, focusing on how to define re-usable chunks of data, and modeling a wide variety of related messages as combinations of those chunks.

Agility was achieved by the DSH by defining singular (less flexible) messages first and directly storing those, with only minimal modifications to tag them with additional service data and remove personal information.

NoSQL technology alters the overall architecture

A key observation from this work is that NoSQL technology does not "plug in" to an existing architecture as a persistence alternative in place of a relational database. Instead, the overall nature of the architecture - starting with data architecture and system architecture but extending also to enterprise architecture – must change when NoSQL technologies are used.

The author's experience is that this shift is challenging to navigate, and ideally these examples illustrate the different concerns and approaches that become paramount when the data models can naturally and easily cross "layer cake" boundaries – that is, when XML or JSON are used for messaging and can also be persisted (approximately) as-is. "Standard" techniques such as logical models and complex transforms or mapping technologies among relational, object and message formats no longer need to be the focus of architecture, and data re-use and re-packaging of existing XML or JSON structures rise to the fore. [1]

References

[Hunt14] Your API versioning is wrong, which is why I decided to do it 3 different wrong ways. (2014) From blog post.

[Rayfield12] Sports Refresh: Dynamic Semantic Publishing. (2012) From BBC blog post.

[Yourdon79] Edward Yourdon, Larry Constantine. (1979) ISBN:0138544719. Prentice-Hall, Inc. *Structured Design: Fundamentals of a Discipline of Computer Program and Systems Design.*

[Chessell15] Mandy Chessell, Gandhi Sivakumar, Dan Wolfson, Kerard Hogg, Ray Harishankar. (2015). ISBN:0-13-336634-0. IBM Press. *Common Information Models for an Open, Analytical, and Agile World.*

[Time14] Steven Brill. (2014) 183(9). *Time Magazine*. "Obama's Trauma Team".

---

[1] Note that workarounds and re-mappings can be introduced, where older message formats are supported even as new formats are created. Troy Hunt discusses some issues with trying to manage multiple formats simultaneously in a blog post on API Versioning at Hunt14. See Yourdon and Constantine: Yourdon79 with full chapters on coupling and cohesion, respectively. We are using simplified, "notional" documents in this paper, meaning the documents have the same basic structure as actual documents in the described systems, but the exact structure, element names and namespaces are not used.

Damon Feldman
Solutions Director
MarkLogic Corporation

Damon Feldman is a passionate "Mark-Logician," having been with the company for over 7 years as it has evolved into the company it is today. He has worked on or led some of the largest MarkLogic projects in terms of both volume of data and complexity of implementation, for customers ranging from the US Intelligence Community to HealthCare.gov to private insurance companies.

Balisage Series on Markup Technologies

XML In, Web Out: International Symposium on sub rosa XML
Proceedings

XSLT as a Modern, Powerful Static Website Generator

Publishing Hogrefe's Clinical Handbook of Psychotropic Drugs as a Web App

Martin Kraetke
Lead Content Engineer
le-tex publishing services GmbH

Gerrit Imsieke
Managing Director
le-tex publishing services GmbH

XML In, Web Out: International Symposium on sub rosa XML
August 1, 2016

Copyright © 2016 by the authors. All rights reserved.

How to cite this paper

Kraetke, Martin, and Gerrit Imsieke. "XSLT as a Modern, Powerful Static Website Generator: Publishing Hogrefe's Clinical Handbook of Psychotropic Drugs as a Web App." Presented at XML In, Web Out: International Symposium on sub rosa XML, Washington, DC, August 1, 2016. In *Proceedings of XML In, Web Out: International Symposium on sub rosa XML*. Balisage Series on Markup Technologies, vol. 18 (2016). DOI: 10.4242/BalisageVol18.Kraetke02.

Abstract

In scientific, technical, and medical (STM) publishing, XML is a common data format for typeset products. Electronic renditions are regularly created from these XML sources, too. However, these HTML renderings are mainly considered as an alternative rendering with no added value, and most users of STM literature still consume the content in PDF format or on paper. Hogrefe Publishing decided to market its flagship reference product, the Clinical Handbook of Psychotropic Drugs, as a standalone electronic version. The electronic version should offer quicker lookups by several criteria, such as substance name, trade name, indication, and interaction. In addition, it should be mobile-friendly so that healthcare professionals can use their mobile phones to access the content, including large tables.

Although single-source publishing in STM is not considered a "sub rosa" application of XML at all, there are remarkably few known examples of standalone, enriched Web applications that are derived from a printed reference work and published in parallel. This paper argues that this kind of application can be created from XML with relatively moderate effort using modern XSLT versions and that this approach is superior to what has recently become popular for content-driven Web sites – Markdown content and static site generators written in procedural languages.

Table of Contents

Introduction

Markup
Web Application
Navigation
Mobile First
Offline First
Page Generation
Outlook
Conclusion

Introduction

Hogrefe's Clinical Handbook of Psychotropic Drugs (CHPD) is a standard reference work that is particularly popular among North American mental health professionals. It is organized by indication groups such as psychosis or depression. It contains many tables with dosing information, trade names, etc.

Supplemented by patient information sheets, the volume comprises about 400 pages (A4 paper size, landscape orientation, spiral binding, see Figure 1).

Figure 1

Irreversible Monoamine Oxidase Inhibitors (cont.)

Class of Drug	Example	Interaction Effects
Sympathomimetic amine	Indirect acting: amphetamine, methylphenidate, ephedrine, pseudoephedrine, phenylpropanolamine, dopamine, tyramine	Release of large amounts of norepinephrine with hypertensive reaction; AVOID
	Direct acting: epinephrine, isoproterenol, norepinephrine (levarterenol), methoxamine, salbutamol	No interaction
	Phenylephrine	Increased pressor response
Tetrabenazine		Central excitatory syndrome and hypertension reported due to central and peripheral release of catecholamines
Triptan	Sumatriptan, zolmitriptan, rizatriptan	Serotonin syndrome (see p. 8); AVOID; recommended that 2 weeks elapse after discontinuing an irreversible MAOI before using sumatriptan

Monoamine Oxidase B Inhibitor

Product Availability*

Chemical Class	Generic Name	Trade Name	Dosage Forms and Strengths
Levo acetylenic derivative of phenethylamine	Selegiline (deprenyl) transdermal(B)	EMSAM	Transdermal patch: 20 mg/20 cm², 30 mg/30 cm², 40 mg/40 cm² that deliver on average 6 mg/24 h, 9 mg/24 h, 12 mg/24 h

* Refer to Health Canada's Drug Product Database or the FDA's Drugs@FDA for the most current availability information, (B) Not marketed in Canada

Indications‡

- (approved) Major depressive disorder (MDD) in adults
- Cocaine use: Selegiline may reduce physiological and subjective effects

General Comments

- Approved in low doses of oral formulation (Canada and USA) for the treatment of Parkinson's disease; higher doses required for treatment of MDD
- Transdermal patches contain 1 mg of selegiline per cm² and deliver approximately 0.3 mg of selegiline per cm² over 24 h

Pharmacology

- Transdermal selegiline leads to sustained plasma concentrations of the parent compound, increasing the amount of drug delivered to the brain and decreasing metabolite production. At low doses, selegiline irreversibly inhibits MAO-B, which is involved in oxidative deamination of dopamine in the brain and also inhibits the uptake of dopamine. At higher doses, it inhibits both MAO-A and B. The transdermal formulation allows for targeted inhibition of central nervous system MAO-A and MAO-B with minimal effects on MAO-A in the GI (gut wall) and hepatic systems (avoids first pass effect), thereby reducing the risk of interactions with tyramine-rich foods
- Induces antioxidant enzymes and decreases the formation of oxygen radicals; it interferes with early apoptotic signaling events induced by various kinds of insults in cell cultures, thus protecting cells from apoptotic death

‡ Indications listed here do not necessarily apply to all countries. Please refer to a country's regulatory database (e.g., US Federal Drug Administration, Health Canada Drug Product Database) for the most current availability information and indications

Dosing

- See p. 64
- EMSAM should be applied to dry, intact skin on the upper torso (below the neck and above the waist), upper thigh or the outer surface of the upper arm once every 24 h
- 20 mg/20 cm² delivers 6 mg/24 h – found effective in MDD without the need for dietary restrictions; if dose increases are indicated for individual patients, they should occur in dose increments of 3 mg/24 h (up to a maximum dose of 12 mg/24 h) at intervals of no less than 2 weeks
- Recommended dose for elderly patients is 6 mg/24 h
- No adjustment in dosage necessary in moderate hepatic or renal insufficiency

Pharmacokinetics

- See p. 64
- Following dermal application of EMSAM to humans, 25–30% of the selegiline content, on average, is delivered systemically over 24 h (range ~ 10–40%). Transdermal dosing results in substantially higher exposure to selegiline and lower exposure to metabolites compared to oral dosing, where extensive first-pass metabolism occurs. Absorption of selegiline is similar when EMSAM is applied to the upper torso or upper thigh; it is not metabolized in human skin
- Selegiline is approximately 90% bound to plasma protein
- Steady-state selegiline plasma concentrations achieved within 5 days of daily dosing
- Extensively metabolized by several CYP450 enzymes including CYP2B6, CYP2C9, and CYP3A4/5 and CYP2A6
- Selegiline and N-desmethylselegiline cause a concentration-dependent inhibition of CYP2D6 at 10–250 μM and CYP3A4/5 at 25–250 μM and have a minor effect on CYP2C19 and CYP2B6
- Mean half-lives of selegiline and its three metabolites, R(–)-N-desmethylselegiline, R(–)-amphetamine, and R(–)-methamphetamine, range from 18 to 25 h
- No pharmacokinetic information is available on selegiline or its metabolites in patients with renal or hepatic impairment

Adverse Effects

- See p. 61
- Insomnia common (can be lessened by taking the patch off before bedtime)
- Dermatological reactions common at site of application of patch (24%) (rotate sites of application)
- Diarrhea, pharyngitis, dizziness, lightheadedness, headache (18%), hypotension (10%), dry mouth
- Increased blood pressure at doses above 6 mg/24 h possible
- Increased anxiety, agitation, irritability, increase in suicidal thoughts; activation of mania/hypomania (0.4%)
- Weight loss > 5% body weight (5%)

Contraindications

- Simultaneous administration of drugs with serotonergic properties (see Interactions, p. 56)
- Combination with sympathomimetic amines, including amphetamines as well as cold products and weight-reducing preparations that contain vasoconstrictors

Precautions

- Though dietary restrictions are not required for the 6 mg/24 h dose, use of higher doses can negate drug selectivity and pressor response can occur to tyramine-rich foods – patients should observe dietary and drug restrictions (as per irreversible MAO inhibitors pp. 51–52)
- A 14-day washout is required between termination of selegiline and starting an antidepressant with serotonergic activity, to prevent serotonin syndrome (see Interactions p. 13 and Switching Antidepressants pp. 65–66)
- Both adults and children may experience worsening of their MDD, unusual changes in their behavior, and/or the emergence of suicidal ideation and behavior
- Patients should be evaluated carefully for a history of drug abuse, and such patients should be observed closely for signs of EMSAM misuse or abuse (e.g., development of tolerance, increases in dose, or drug-seeking behavior)

Toxicity

- CNS and cardiovascular toxicity likely
- Delays of up to 12 h between ingestion of drug and the appearance of signs may occur, and peak effects may not be observed for 24–48 h. Since death has been reported following overdosage with MAOI agents, hospitalization with close monitoring during this period is essential

Management

- Symptomatic and supportive

In addition to the main work, which is currently published in its 21st edition, Hogrefe publishes a derivative work that covers psychotropic drugs for children and adolescents. New editions of each volume are published every other year, in an alternating fashion.

The print editions have been published from XML source in a bespoke vocabulary by another typesetter for years when the publisher started exploring the feasibility of an online edition. le-tex was tasked with analyzing the existing XML. It turned out that particularly the table markup was insufficient for reflowable rendering, as it aligned paragraphs in adjacent columns based upon their print line count. In a Web rendering with user-adjustable font sizes and dynamic column widths, paragraphs don't necessarily keep their print line count. This will lead to misaligned table rows. In order to fix this and other markup issues, le-tex recommended that the vocabulary be switched to something more common and suggested that DocBook 5 with HTML tables be used.

Markup

The markup is DocBook 5 with some conventions and one minor extension. The extension is that a `linkends` attribute may be used in citations, allowing a space separated list of target references to be cited. This in turn allows for a selective rendering for print (for example, "[3–5,7]") and online (linked individual numbers, "[3,4,5,7]"). The print edition is typeset with LaTeX that is natively able to group adjacent citation numbers from a raw list.

A convention has been established for marking up print-only and Web-only content. This distinction is necessary for front matter content in that there is a different "about the book" page for print and Web and the Web rendering of the patient information sheets (PIS) consists of only the heading and a link to the corresponding PDF. This is because the PIS are meant for printing them out. The DocBook attribute `condition="web|print"` was used to mark up rendering-specific content. This use is in line with DocBook's guidelines that don't make any assumptions on which values this attribute may assume.

Although the print edition contains a combined index, the different indexterm types are encoded using the standard `role` attribute. Its values are 'indication' and 'tradename', while entries without `role` attribute are considered as generic (substance) names. Some of the generic names are additionally classified (using the `type` attribute) as being main entries, that is, the primary location where a substance is described. These locations are rendered boldface in the printed index.

The DocBook source data is distributed over 30 files that are consolidated into a wrapper file using XInclude. The XML sources comprise 5 Megabytes.

Web Application

Navigation

In addition to a table-of-contents naviagation, the Web application includes these indexes (Generic Names, Trade Names, Indications, Interacting Agents) as primary navigation widgets. In addition, there is an auto-complete search form that is configured with the list of index terms. When the user enters a search term or clicks on the corresponding index term in the alphabetically grouped indexes, a pre-generated search result list is displayed. If the search terms are generic names, the results are clasified according to the color scheme of the book, as displayed in Figure 2 (green for pharmacology & dosing, red for admonitions, blue for indications, trade names, and other general information, orange for information pertaining to special patient groups such as pregnant women).

Figure 2

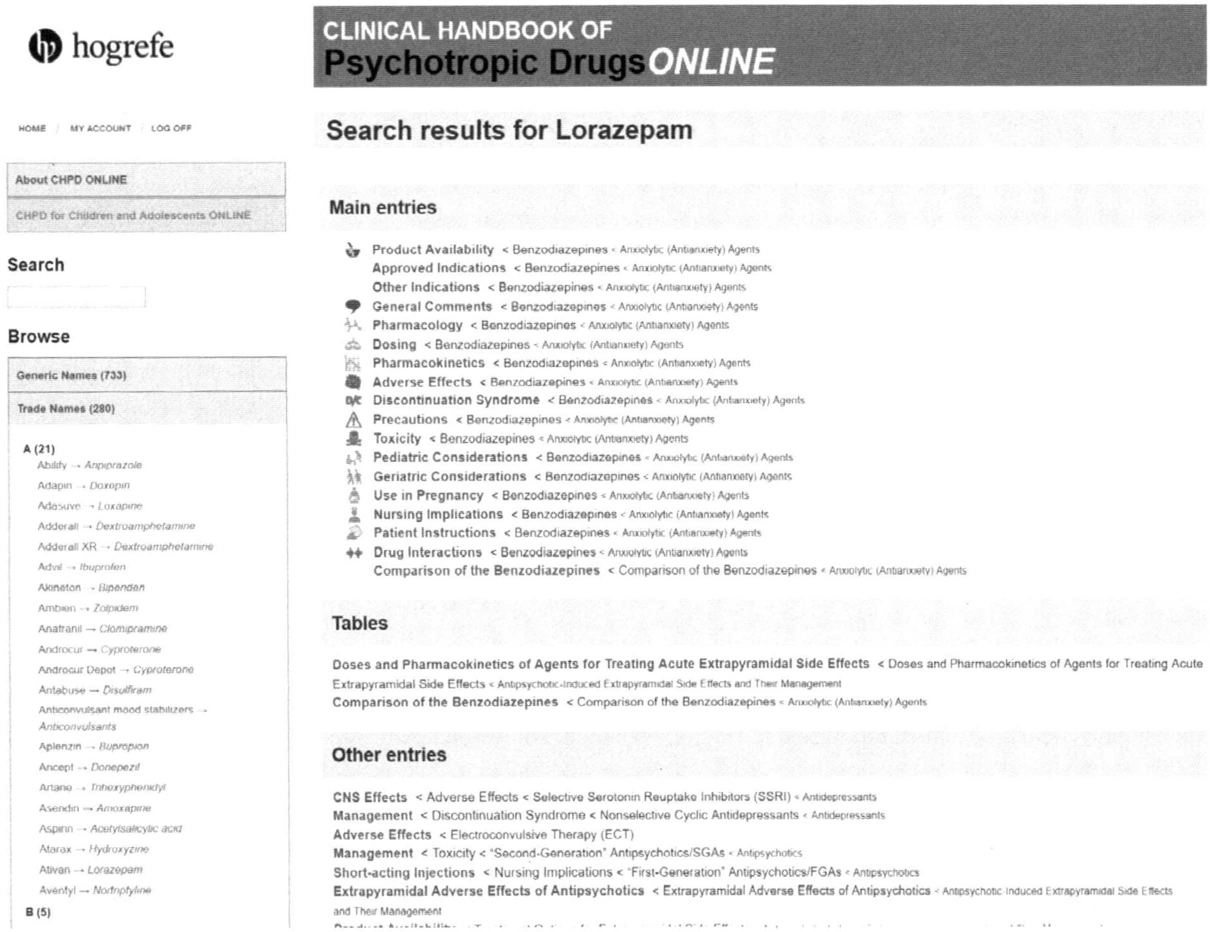

A search result page

> ***Note***
>
> The search result lists could be extended to a complete full-text index, excluding stop words, but this was not deemed to add much value.

Search result lists display the main entries in first place. These are often different sections of the same chapter, since the book is organized by substance classes. After that, occurrences in tables are displayed. If Javascript is enabled, the search term is highlighted on the target page when following a link from a search result page (Figure 3).

Figure 3

	moderate impairment – reducing dose by 50% recommended, contraindicated in severe impairment								
Lorazepam (Ativan)	Oral: Up to 2 mg qid Sublingual: 1–2 mg up to tid IM: 1–2 mg for dystonia Renal impairment: No adjustment Hepatic impairment: mild to moderate – no adjustment; severe impairment – use caution	Oral: 15–30 min	Oral: 2 h Sublingual: 1 h IM: <3 h	90%	88–92%; free fraction may be significantly higher in the elderly	10–20 h; 32–70 h (end-stage renal disease)	Urine(88% as inactive metabolites); feces (7%)	UGT2B7, UGT2B15	–
Clonazepam (Rivotril, Klonopin)	Oral: 0.5–6 mg/day in divided doses	15–30 min	1–4 h	90%	86%	17–60 h	Urine (< 2% as unchanged drug)	**3A4** (P)	–

A search result page

If one follows a link to a subsection, the relevant subsection will unfold. The displayed URL will be modified accordingly, using the Javascript `pushState()` method [ref_pushState]. When the user manually unfolds additional subsections, the URL will be modified accordingly (Figure 4). This allows pages with their section expansion state and highlighting to be bookmarked and to passed on as links. This way, the drawback of many single-page apps, which is insufficient bookmarkability, can be avoided.

> ***Note***
>
> Both the expansion state and the search terms to be highlighted are encoded in the query string of the URL, by means of said `pushState()` Javascript method. When such a URL, for example `benzodiazepines.html?sections=d2e99762,d2e101505&term=Lorazepam`, is accessed later, the HTML page loads with all subsections initially collapsed. A client-side Javascript routine then looks for headings with the corresponding IDs (`d2e99762` and `d2e101505` in this example) and toggles the visibility of the HTML content that is in the same `<div>` as the heading.
>
> Another client-side Javascript routine analyzes the `term` part of the query string (for example, `...&term=Lorazepam`) searches the text for occurrences of the search term and injects HTML `<span>`s with a CSS class that effects the yellow highlighting.

It should be noted that in the absence of Javascript, users can still bookmark whole sections (read: HTML pages) according to their plain URLs. It won't be possible to save the expansion state though. This provides graceful degradation for when client-side scripting is unavailable.

Figure 4

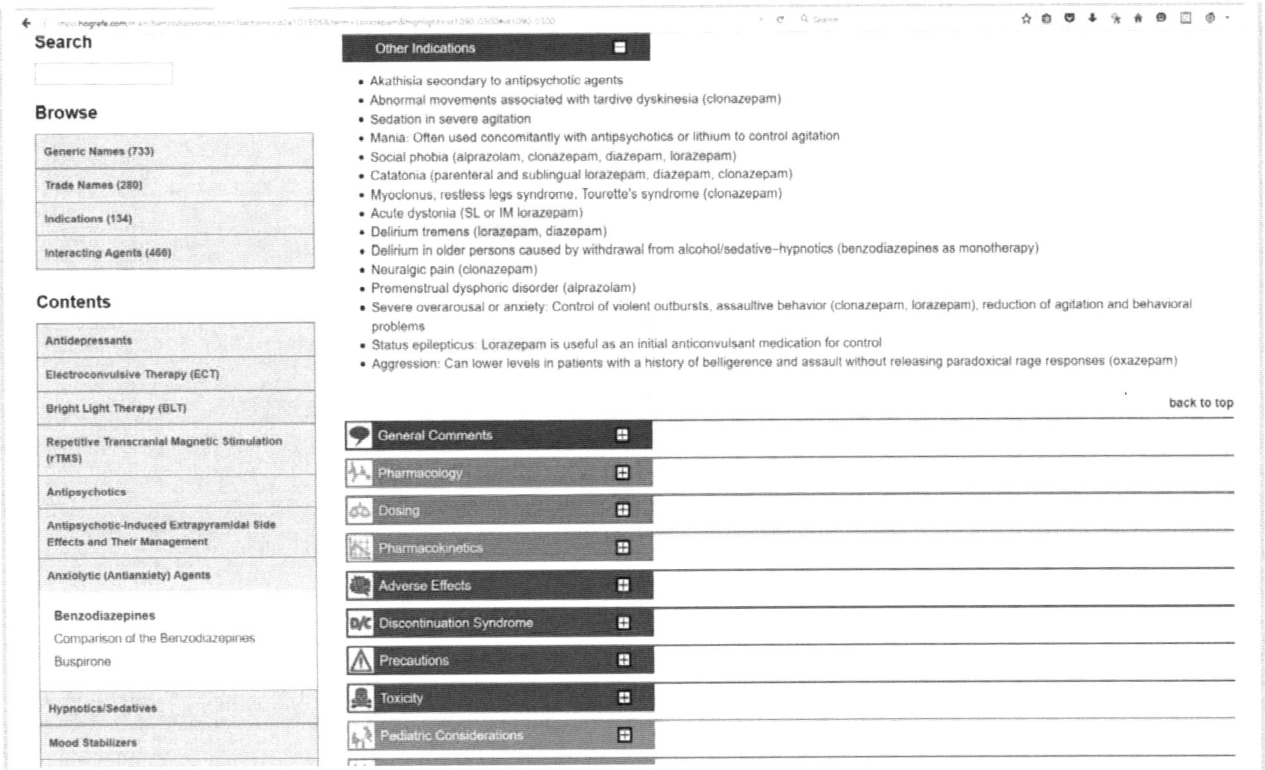

Following a link will unfold its HTML section and modify the displayed URL

Mobile First

Since Hogrefe found out that many healthcare professionals wanted to use the site on their mobile devices, a responsive layout using media queries was established shortly after launching the Web app. However, there were still many large tables that were too wide for mobile displays. Several solutions have been evaluated, among them also CSS-only solutions that switched to a list view for mobile. However, it was decided that a tabular view was still preferable on mobile. In addition, some tables were even too wide for desktop screens. Hogrefe then commissioned development of a Javascript-based table widget that allows users to selectively collapse columns and rows [ref_tableWidget]. The resulting user experience can be seen in Figure 5.

Figure 5

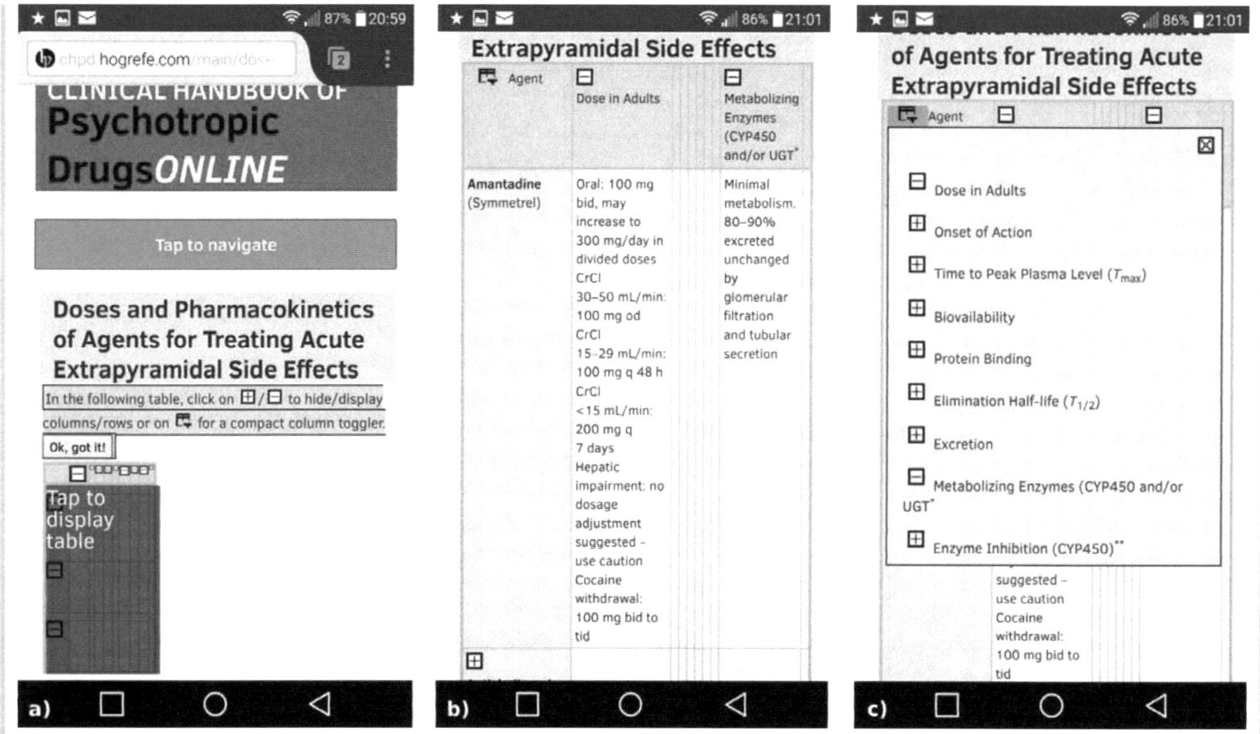

Table widget on mobile devices. a) Initial view. b) View with some columns and a row in collapsed state. c) A flyout menu allows toggling for columns that are outside the viewport

Offline First

The Web application may be run either standalone or within a web application server that primarily is responsible for enforcing access control. It should be noted that even the autocomplete search runs offline since it is Javascript-based, as do other features such as URI rewriting for bookmarking the expansion state of subsections. The Web application may be distributed on a USB stick and run from there.

Page Generation

As stated above, the application runs on static pages. Everything, including a JSON list of search terms and the search result pages, is generated by a static site generator. Static site generators have become a hot topic particularly for powering large, content-driven, high-traffic Web properties [ref_static]. The article discusses that the number of static site generators on Github has more than doubled during 2015. Technology-wise, most of the generators seem to be written in procedural languages such as Ruby or Javascript. Often they operate on Markdown, YAML or HTML content and use more or less established templating languages.[1]

CHPD's static site generator is XSLT 2.0 which is not only a standardized templating language but also a very powerful one (see Figure 6). It renders the DocBook input to HTML, chunking at appropriate locations. In addition to this, it may easily create the index navigation. In contrast to text-based input that needs to be parsed and queried by custom program logic, the XML input may be easily queried using XPath. This allows for a really straightforward processing step that first selects the indexterms of a certain `role`, then calculates custom sort keys (e.g., β is sorted as "beta") and then groups the items according to their initial letters.

In total, more than 1400 pages are being generated, of which approx. 1100 are search result pages.

Figure 6

```
<xsl:template name="search-results">
  <xsl:variable name="indexterms" select=".//indexterm[not(see)]" as="element(indexterm)*" />
  <xsl:variable name="distinct" select="distinct-values($indexterms/primary)" />
  <xsl:message>Distinct primary entries: <xsl:value-of select="count($distinct)"/>
  </xsl:message>
  <xsl:for-each-group select="$distinct" group-by="letex:normalize-string-for-filename(.)">
    <xsl:sort/>
    <xsl:variable name="indexterms" select="key('proper-indexterms', current-group()[1], $root)" />
    <xsl:variable name="rendered-term" select="letex:specify-term($indexterms[1])" />
    <xsl:if test="count(current-group()) gt 1">
      <xsl:message>Multiple forms of index term <xsl:value-of select="current-grouping-key()"/>:
      <xsl:value-of select="string-join(current-group(), '; ')"/>
      </xsl:message>
    </xsl:if>
    <xsl:variable name="html-title" as="xs:string">
      <xsl:value-of select="$rendered-term"/>
    </xsl:variable>
    <xsl:result-document href="{$outputdir}/s_{current-grouping-key()}.html">
      <xsl:for-each select="$root">
        <xsl:choose>
          <!-- application = true: output only inner content div container for normal html pages -->
          <xsl:when test="$application eq 'true'">
            <xsl:call-template name="html-body">
              <xsl:with-param name="title" select="$html-title" tunnel="yes"/>
              <xsl:with-param name="h1" tunnel="yes">
                <xsl:apply-templates select="$indexterms[1]" mode="indexterm-as-heading" />
              </xsl:with-param>
              <xsl:with-param name="current-page" select="()" tunnel="yes"/>
              <xsl:with-param name="bodynodes" select="letex:indexterm-overview( $indexterms, $indexterms[1]/primary )"
                tunnel="yes" />
            </xsl:call-template>
          </xsl:when>
```

An XSLT snippet that is responsible for search result page generation

It should be noted that the same expressive power and elegance was not available with XSLT 1 for at least four reasons:

- XSLT 1 did not provide a standard chunking (result document) mechanism;
- The XSLT 2 conversion stylesheet provides and uses 20 custom XPath functions that encapsulate calculations and help cut down the complexity of XPath expressions, thereby greatly improving maintainability. Custom `xsl:function`s are not available in XSLT 1;
- XSLT 2 provides native grouping instructions;
- The conversion stylesheet heavily uses regular expression functions that are not available in XSLT 1. This is a bit counterintuitive as one would not expect many regex-based text manipulations when rendering DocBook to HTML. Analysis shows that they are primarily used for file path manipulations and in sort key normalizations, for example replacing α with `alpha` or the space character class `\p{Zs}` with a plain space.

There are workarounds for these operations in XSLT 1. However, they tend to be verbose and less maintainable.

Outlook

Hogrefe plans to migrate all content to a BITS-based XML dialect called HoBoTS [ref_bits, ref_hobots] that they selected for encoding all of the books they publish.[2] For CHPD, this means that there has to be an XSLT that converts from DocBook to BITS/HoBoTS.

Hogrefe intends to deliver all of their book content on the Atypon Literatum [ref_literatum] platform. The major advantage is that they don't have to run a separate access control application for CHPD. It remains to be seen, however, whether Literatum offers the same set of features that the current Web app provides, particularly with respect to custom indexes and table rendering, but also with respect to the color coding scheme that CHPD users have become used to and that is uniform across the print and the current Web editions.

Conclusion

XSLT 2.0 provides a powerful and standardized way to generate HTML from XML and to create additional navigational structures. The advantage of XSLT was particularly obvious when the responsive layout necessitated structural changes within the generated HTML. Adapting the generating XSLT was a matter of an hour; generating all 1400 pages afresh was a matter of a minute. With HTML5 serialization support introduced in version 3.0, XSLT/XPath is still the processing tool of choice for creating modern Web pages or E-Books from a common XML source.

References

[ref_pushState] "Manipulating the browser history – Adding and modifying history entries". Mozilla Developer Network. [accessed 2016-04-20]. https://developer.mozilla.org/en-US/docs/Web/API/History_API#Adding_and_modifying_history_entries

[ref_tableWidget] Vonende, Mathias; Imsieke, Gerrit: "jquery-tablemanager plugin". [accessed 2016-04-20]. https://github.com/maze-le/jquery-tablemanager

[ref_static] Biilmann Christensen, Mathias: "Why Static Website Generators Are The Next Big Thing". Smashing Magazine. [accessed 2016-04-20]. https://www.smashingmagazine.com/2015/11/modern-static-website-generators-next-big-thing/

[ref_bits] "Book Interchange Tag Set: JATS Extension". [accessed 2016-04-20]. http://jats.nlm.nih.gov/extensions/bits/

[ref_hobots] Imsieke, Gerrit: "Hogrefe Book Tag Set (HoBoTS)". [accessed 2016-04-20]. https://hobots.hogrefe.com/schema/hobots.rng

[ref_literatum] Atypon Systems, Inc.: "Literatum". [accessed 2016-04-20]. https://www.atypon.com/products/literatum/

---

[1] It should be noted that neither Markdown/CommonMark, YAML, or HTML support index terms which are a concept that was fundamental to providing a multi-faceted navigational and search access. These markup deficiencies, combined with the lack of a standardized query language in the text-based formats, makes processing these formats with these procedural languages significantly harder, compared to an XML/XSLT approach.

[2] They decided for a JATS-based vocabulary over DocBook because it shares much of its vocabulary with Hogrefe's journals. The journal XML has always been NLM/JATS based. However, when the CHPD XML was converted to DocBook, BITS was not available yet and there was no canonical way to encode book chapters or index terms in the NLM/JATS family of XML vocabularies. Therefore, DocBook seemed like a good fit at that time.

Martin Kraetke
Lead Content Engineer
le-tex publishing services GmbH

Martin Kraetke is Lead Content Engineer at le-tex publishing services.

Gerrit Imsieke
Managing Director
le-tex publishing services GmbH

Gerrit Imsieke is managing director of le-tex publishing services.

Balisage Series on Markup Technologies

Link to the Balisage Proceedings Home Page at http://www.balisage.net/Proceedings
Link to this paper (entry page with links) at http://www.balisage.net/Proceedings/vol18/html/Murray01/BalisageVol18-Murray01.html

XML In, Web Out: International Symposium on sub rosa XML
Proceedings

XQuery is not (just) a query language: Web application development with XQuery

Gregory Murray
Director of Academic Technology and Digital Scholarship Services
Princeton Theological Seminary
<gregory.murray@ptsem.edu>

XML In, Web Out: International Symposium on sub rosa XML
August 1, 2016

Copyright © 2016, Gregory P. Murray. Released under a Creative Commons Attribution 4.0 International License (CC BY 4.0).

How to cite this paper

Murray, Gregory. "XQuery is not (just) a query language: Web application development with XQuery." Presented at XML In, Web Out: International Symposium on sub rosa XML, Washington, DC, August 1, 2016. In *Proceedings of XML In, Web Out: International Symposium on sub rosa XML*. Balisage Series on Markup Technologies, vol. 18 (2016). DOI: 10.4242/BalisageVol18.Murray01.

Abstract

XQuery is widely known as a query language for XML, but it's also a full-fledged, functional programming language which, with a limited number of implementation-provided extensions, can serve in a web development context as both the query language and the programming language. When you have data in XML form that needs to be delivered in some way on the web, using XQuery as the server-side programming language has significant practical advantages. After briefly describing those advantages, this paper will lay out techniques for developing web applications in XQuery—techniques that will reduce complexity and help developers produce well-organized, testable, portable code that will be comparatively easy to build upon and maintain over time. Topics include using MVC, keeping functions testable, and facilitating code portability by using available standardizations like RESTXQ and by isolating implementation-specific functions into separate modules.

Table of Contents

Preface: Limitations of the SQL analogy
Advantages of XQuery for web delivery of XML content
Techniques for web application development with XQuery
- Utilizing MVC
  - Model
  - View
  - Controller
  - Ancillary modules
- Keeping functions testable
- Improving code portability and sharing
  - Using available standardizations
  - Isolating implementation-specific functions

Conclusion

Preface: Limitations of the SQL analogy

XQuery is widely known as a query language for XML. In the domain of web application development—where the classic technology stack is a relational database accessible via SQL paired with one of several popular programming languages (Java, .NET languages, Perl, PHP, Python, Ruby, etc.)—there is far less awareness that XQuery is actually a full-fledged, functional programming language. Even less recognized is the fact that XQuery, with a limited number of implementation-provided extensions, can serve in a web development context as both the database query language and the server-side programming language. When describing XQuery to web developers or project managers accustomed to the classic technology stack, it is tempting to define XQuery in a way that someone in that context can easily latch onto: XQuery is to XML databases as SQL is to relational databases. This commonplace analogy seems harmless enough initially, but it is actually misleading and counter-productive if it is not immediately qualified and expanded. Defining XQuery as a query language for XML is the truth but not the whole truth. When you have data in XML form that needs to be delivered in some way on the web, using XQuery as the server-side programming language has significant practical advantages. After briefly describing those advantages, this paper will lay out techniques for developing web applications in XQuery—techniques that can reduce complexity and help developers produce well-organized, testable, portable code that will be comparatively easy to build upon and maintain over time.

Advantages of XQuery for web delivery of XML content

XQuery is specifically designed to work hand-in-glove with XML data natively. There is no need to provide a mapping between the data and the programming language, such as the "object-relational mapping" that is inherently necessary when working in an object-oriented programming language in conjunction with a relational database. In fact, the need for such a mapping is not limited to relational data; an analogous kind of mapping—let's call it an "object-document mapping"—is equally necessary when using an object-oriented language to work with data in XML form. Whether relational or XML-based, the data model still has to be translated or mapped to the facilities and affordances of the programming language. The one is not inherently designed to work with the other, and in fact the data and the language collide in a "clash of paradigms" (Seiferle, p. 20), resulting in the so-called "impedance mismatch" (Kaufmann, §1; Seiferle, p. 20-21). This gap between the data and the language must be bridged, adding a layer of complexity to the technology stack of the web application. With XQuery, there is no data-language gap and therefore no bridge.

If you don't need a bridge, then you don't need a web development framework (Ruby on Rails, CakePHP, Django, etc.) to provide it. Although such frameworks usually provide services in addition to object-relational mapping (scaffolding, templating, etc.; Seiferle, p. 3-4), all things considered, eschewing these frameworks actually provides real advantages by entirely sidestepping layers of complexity that frameworks can only hide, not eliminate (Seiferle, p. 22). Not only do such frameworks lock developers into the assumptions and requirements the framework espouses, they also invariably evolve over time, sometimes rapidly. Sooner or later it becomes necessary to upgrade the framework itself, either because there is a compelling reason (such as a new feature or a needed bug fix) or because there is an absolute necessity (such as a show-stopping incompatibility between the framework and a change to the environment, like a newer version of the database server, programming language or operating system). The inherent technological complexity and multiple moving parts of any given web development framework can end up putting developers into a hamster's wheel of release notes, upgrades, deprecated features, and incompatibilities—all of which add up to time spent on mere maintenance rather than intentional refactoring or development of new or improved functionality. By contrast, the core XML-related specifications—including XQuery and its accompanying and supporting specs—have proven exceptionally stable. Their evolution has been characterized not only by infrequent updates but also by a high degree of backward compatibility.

The differences between these technology stacks have concrete, real-world consequences. Using a language designed for the data it is working with, thereby avoiding "the technology jungle of mixing different technologies and data models" (Kaufmann, §7), prevents a good deal of mundane work and frees developers to focus on the domain and goals of the application rather than an ever-changing web development environment.

Techniques for web application development with XQuery

Utilizing MVC

Despite the drawbacks of web development frameworks just described, there is one common feature that is just as relevant for XQuery web development as for any other language: the utilization of MVC (model, view, controller). There are countless readily available resources of varying depth, from books to blog posts, that describe MVC, including and especially in the domain of web application development, where the use of MVC has become wildly popular since the advent of Ruby on Rails. The problem is that as a concept MVC is general and flexible enough to allow many possible variations when the concept is put into practice. Various methodologies have proliferated, leaving the whole idea of MVC seeming rather arcane to the uninitiated—and to the initiated, for that matter. (As the adage goes, ask five web developers how they use MVC and you'll get six different answers.) MVC is commonly called an "architecture," but that term is already overburdened and therefore unilluminating. However, much of this confusion is unnecessary, because in its essence MVC is just a technique for organizing code, with the principal goal being the classic "separation of concerns" whereby presentation code has no knowledge of how data is stored and accessed, and database-related code has no knowledge of how data is presented to the user.

If for now we set aside the variations and elaborations of MVC, a few core principles remain. Models understand how data is represented (modeled) and handle database interaction. Views construct the presentation of data to the user. Controllers receive input and respond accordingly, utilizing models and views to do so.

Admittedly this (deliberately minimal) definition leaves out some important decisions. Any non-trivial web application will need multiple views, but some variations of MVC allow, or even require, multiple controllers or multiple models. Other methodologies differ as to which MVC component(s) can or cannot call upon the model for database interaction. Some web development frameworks, and indeed some web developers themselves, can be quite puristic about these differentiations, but stridency in this context is unhelpful. How exactly to organize code within an MVC approach should be based more on the nature and goals of a particular web application than on abstract principles. A more complex application may merit a more complex use of the MVC components. This is not to say that we should be lax or inconsistent in our implementation of MVC, only that we should select an MVC methodology based on practical considerations. To get started with MVC, there is nothing wrong with having one controller and one model, along with a view for each main kind of HTTP response the application provides.

The modular nature of XQuery lends itself easily and directly to the MVC concept. Each model, view, and controller is implemented as an XQuery library module.

Model

The model is responsible for interacting with the database; no other component should create, read, update or delete data (think "no CRUD outside the model"). In this sense it acts as a kind of API (or like an encapsulated object, in object-oriented terms), which other modules call upon without needing to know anything about the database or how to interact with it. Ideally this separation of concerns is enforced to the point that one could swap out the underlying database server for a different one without touching any code in the controller(s) or views. (Conversely, we should be able to overhaul the presentation or adjust business logic without touching any code in the model(s).)

However, in the context of this discussion, in which data is in XML form, there is an important additional consideration. We have to decide whether the model should not only handle all database interaction but also handle all navigation of the structure of the XML documents, which is to say, whether only the model should contain XPath expressions. This decision is essentially a question of how strictly we want to separate knowledge of the document structure from the knowledge of how the document content should be formatted and presented. For example, let's say we have this kind of markup, containing information about a book:

```
<?xml version="1.0" encoding="UTF-8"?>
<doc>
  <metadata>
    <id>ablgeschichtedes03gind</id>
    <name>Gindely, Anton, 1829-1892</name>
    <title>Geschichte des dreissigjährigen Krieges</title>
    <date>1869</date>
    <language code="de">German</language>
```

```
    <format>Book</format>
    <callNumber source="oclc">D258 .G49</callNumber>
    <class>History</class>
    <topics>
      <topic>Thirty Years' War, 1618-1648</topic>
    </topics>
  </metadata>
</doc>
```

Let's also assume that since the model handles database interaction, we have set up a function named `get-xml-doc` in the model to retrieve from the database any given XML document in its entirety, given its unique identifier. To get values such as book title and author name that we need to display, one option is to allow the presentation code to have knowledge of the document structure and grab the data directly:

```
import module namespace m = "http://balisage.net/ns/Bal2016murr0319/model" at ... ;
...
let $doc := m:get-xml-doc("ablgeschichtedes03gind")
let $title := fn:string($doc/doc/metadata/title)
let $name := fn:string($doc/doc/metadata/name)
```

Alternatively we can require the model alone to have knowledge of document structure and provide functions for retrieving the data from the model. If the model has these functions:

```
module namespace m = "http://balisage.net/ns/Bal2016murr0319/model";

(:~ Returns the book title as a string. :)
declare function m:get-title($doc as document-node())
as xs:string
{
  fn:string($doc/doc/metadata/title)
};

(:~ Returns the author name as a string. :)
declare function m:get-name($doc as document-node())
as xs:string
{
  fn:string($doc/doc/metadata/name)
};
```

then the presentation code doesn't need to carry any knowledge of the document structure:

```
import module namespace m = "http://balisage.net/ns/Bal2016murr0319/model" at ... ;
...
let $doc := m:get-xml-doc("ablgeschichtedes03gind")
let $title := m:get-title($doc)
let $name := m:get-name($doc)
```

In an example this simple, the difference is trivial, but in a real-world web application the XPath expressions will likely be more elaborate as well as broadly distributed throughout a sizable body of presentation code spanning multiple XQuery modules. Moreover, the same XPath expressions will typically be needed more than once throughout the presentation code. Abstracting knowledge of the markup into the model enforces a stricter separation of concerns. With this approach, if the markup schema changes, only the model would need to be refactored, since knowledge of the markup is confined to the model.

As mentioned above, there is nothing inherently wrong with having a single model for a given web application, but there are some use cases for separating database-related code into multiple models. In situations where a web application needs to work with documents in multiple XML markup languages, it might make sense to have a different MVC model (that is, a discrete XQuery module) for each document type. Similarly, if an application includes full-text searching capability, it is logical to group search-related functions into a separate model. This is especially true if your chosen implementation provides its own functions for searching (as opposed to implementing the W3C XQuery Full-Text recommendation), so that in addition to improving code organization per se the search-specific model is isolating implementation-defined functions, to improve code portability and sharing (more on this below).

View

The role of the view is to provide the presentation, whether for human- or machine-readability. For example, a very commonplace pattern (used by all manner of web applications from Amazon to Zappos) is to provide searching, leading to search results, leading to an item-level page showing all relevant information for a particular item. In this approach, the home page containing the search form, the search results page, and the item-level page are separate views, each one implemented as its own XQuery library module (all of which could be grouped in a single `views` directory). In a web application designed for display in a browser, most views will return an HTML document, whereas a web service might return data as JSON or XML, which is nonetheless a view.

Because most web-based user interfaces are designed with shared components such as headers, sidebars and footers, it makes sense to have an XQuery module that serves as a "layout" (or to have multiple layout modules, if more than one page layout is needed within the same application). In this scenario the view constructs one or more HTML elements constituting the main content of a page, then passes the element(s) (such as a <div>) to a function in the layout module, which returns a complete HTML document with the main content inserted in the appropriate place within the encompassing page layout. The view then returns the complete HTML document.

Figure 1

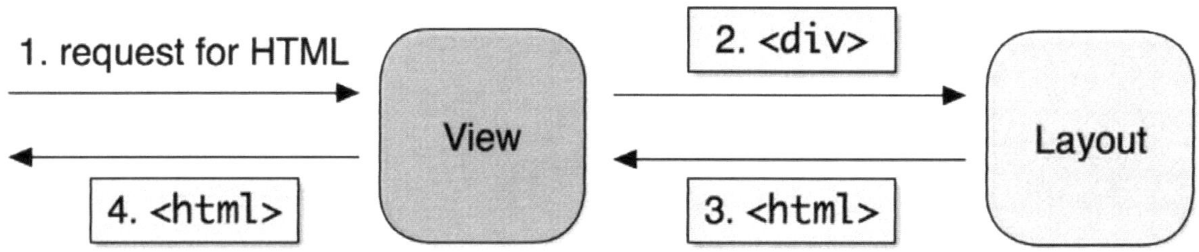

Figure 1: A view utilizing a layout to return a complete HTML document

Controller

The controller is responsible for receiving user input and responding accordingly. It "controls" what happens in response to input and how the model(s) and views are involved in that process. In a web application context, the controller accesses the input from the HTTP request (URL parameters, form data, request headers, cookies) and then calls the appropriate view, as indicated by those input values. Since the XQuery language doesn't provide built-in functions for such HTTP-specific matters, the implementation must supply them, but multiple widely adopted implementations do so. (We will look at some practical examples in BaseX and MarkLogic below.)

Some variations on MVC assert that only the controller should call upon the model to retrieve data, after which the controller passes that data to a view, such that a view never interacts directly with the model.

Figure 2

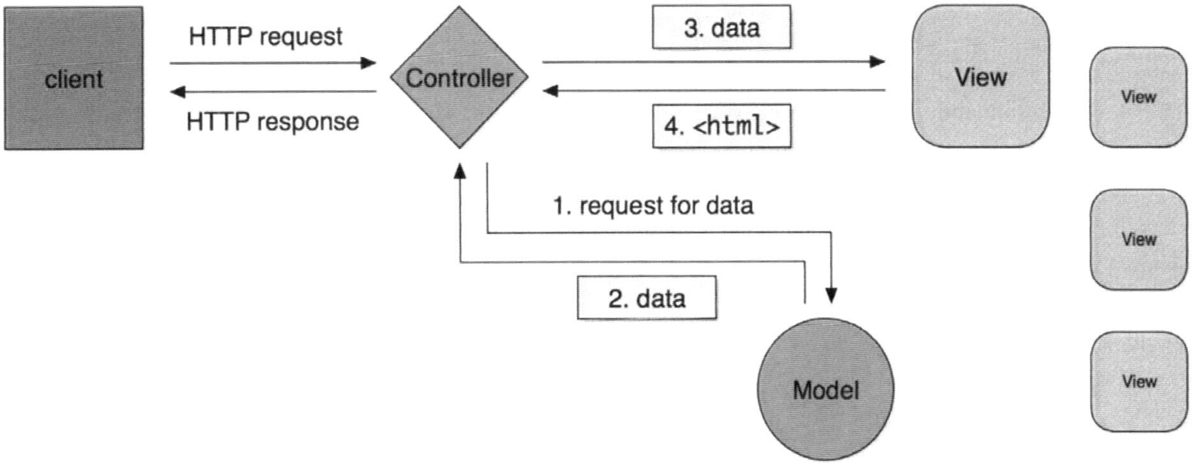

Figure 2: First option: only the controller calls the model

Other MVC variants allow the knowledge of what data is needed by a given view to reside in the view itself, giving it the authority to call the model to get the data it needs to construct a fully formed presentation of that data.

Figure 3

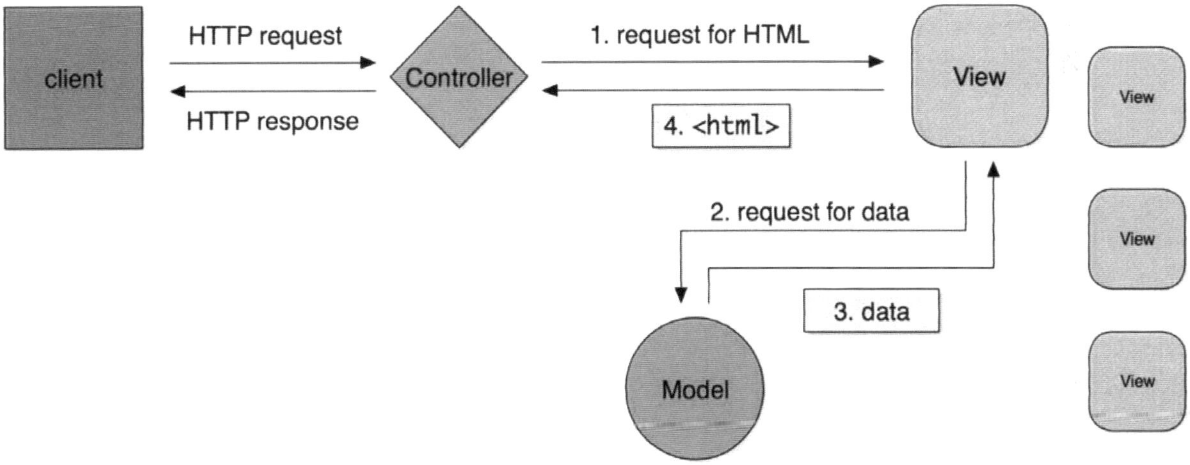

Figure 3: Second option: any given view can call the model

Each approach has its justifications. Each adheres to the principle of the separation of concerns, but in the former method the controller carries the knowledge of what data is needed for each view, while in the latter method the view itself holds that knowledge. In other words, in the first approach the controller is more controlling, and in the second the view is more autonomous and self-aware. (My own preference is for the latter, because it seems reasonable for the view to know what data it needs to display, and because allowing only the controller to request data from the model seems arbitrary. However, I'm only speaking here of retrieving data; when creating/updating/deleting data in the database, the data can and should pass directly from the controller to the model for the insert/update/delete operation, after which the controller calls a "confirmation page" or other appropriate view.)

Ancillary modules

In addition to the core MVC components, additional specialized XQuery library modules are often helpful. A module that acts as a "config file" of global variable declarations allows easy management of settings that might change later or might be needed by multiple modules. Conversely, a "utility" module containing general-purpose, shared functions provides convenience and reduces code duplication. In more complex applications, shared functions that pertain to a particular problem domain or MVC component can be grouped and separated into discrete utility modules.

Keeping functions testable

As shown in Figures 2 and 3 above, when responding to an HTTP request using XQuery and MVC, the chain of processing forms a loop in which the request is routed to the controller, which calls a view, which constructs a fully formatted representation and returns it to the controller, which returns the HTTP response. Throughout this loop, there will be decision points where a given function in a given module must have access to the input values from the HTTP request to make decisions and take actions accordingly. For example, a "search results" view needs to know how the user wants the results sorted, how many results to display at a time, and so on, which can only be known by checking the input from the HTTP request. How best to make those values available throughout the codebase is not inherently obvious. One option is simply to call the implementation-provided functions for accessing these input values wherever such a value is needed. For example, given a URL ending with `?id=abc123` we could do the following:

```
(: MarkLogic example :)
let $id := xdmp:get-request-field("id")
```

```
(: BaseX equivalent of preceding example :)
import module namespace request = "http://exquery.org/ns/request";
...
let $id := request:parameter("id")
```

This approach has a major disadvantage: it leaves implementation-specific function calls strewn throughout the codebase, inhibiting code portability and sharing (more on this below).

A less haphazard technique would be to assign the input values to variables using global (prolog-level) variable declarations in a library module, which could then be imported by any controller or view that needs to access those input values. This module would be similar to the "config file" module mentioned above, but instead of supplying predefined values it would provide values retrieved dynamically from the HTTP request. Let's call it the "parameters" module.

```
(: MarkLogic example :)
(: in the "parameters" module, we put the "id" value in a global variable :)
module namespace params = "http://balisage.net/ns/Bal2016murr0319/parameters";
declare variable $id as xs:string? := xdmp:get-request-field("id");
```

To access those values elsewhere in the codebase, we would simply import the parameters module and reference the relevant variable.

```
(: in the item-level view, we use the previously defined global variable :)
import module namespace params = "http://balisage.net/ns/Bal2016murr0319/parameters" at "parameters.xqy";
...
let $id := $params:id
```

This technique seems reasonable enough and avoids repetitive, dispersed implementation-specific function calls. However, it doesn't solve a deeper problem: functions that access such global variables cannot be independently tested. Unit testing—whereby a single unit of code is tested in isolation from the rest of the program in a deliberately controlled environment, using sample data—is a common and highly advisable practice across many programming domains and languages. In a functional programming language like XQuery, the logical code unit for testing is the function. If a function relies on a global variable containing a value taken from the HTTP request, and if that function gets called (for testing purposes) outside the context of any HTTP request, the value of the global variable will always be empty. Therefore, we have no way to verify the real-world behavior of the function.

This problem can be avoided by providing a function in the controller (since the controller is responsible for receiving user input) that accesses URL parameters or other input values and adds them to an XQuery map (a set of key/value pairs, often called a hash or associative array in other programming languages). The controller can then pass that map to any given view, and each view in turn can pass the map to any functions that need user input values to make determinations about what data is needed, how to format it for display, or other such internal decisions.

```
(: BaseX example :)
```

```
(: In the controller ... :)
module namespace c = "http://balisage.net/ns/Bal2016murr0319/controller";
import module namespace request = "http://exquery.org/ns/request";
import module namespace item = "http://balisage.net/ns/Bal2016murr0319/views/item" at "views/item.xqm";

(:~ Returns a map containing the HTTP request parameters. :)
declare function c:http-params()
as map(*)
{
  map:merge(
    for $name in request:parameter-names()
    let $value := request:parameter($name)
    return map:entry($name, $value)
  )
};

(:~ Calls the appropriate view, based on user input. :)
declare function c:get-view()
as element(html)
{
  (: get HTTP request parameters :)
  let $params := c:http-params()
  return
    if (map:get($params, "id")) then
      (: the presence of "id" indicates that the user is requesting the item-level page for this unique identifier :)
      (: call the item-level view :)
      item:get-html($params)
    else if ... (: call some other view :)
    else if ... (: call some other view :)
    else (: call the view for the home page ... :)
};
```

```
(: In the item-level view ... :)
module namespace item = "http://balisage.net/ns/Bal2016murr0319/views/item";

(:~ Returns a complete HTML document for displaying a given item. :)
declare function item:get-html($params as map(*))
as element(html)
{
  let $id := map:get($params, "id")
  (: build an HTML document for displaying this item, passing $params to other functions as needed ... :)
  (: return HTML ... :)
};
```

To test any given function artificially, outside the context of an actual HTTP request, we can simply construct a map containing sample input and pass it to the function being tested.

```
(: In the testing module ... :)
import module namespace item = "http://balisage.net/ns/Bal2016murr0319/views/item" at "../views/item.xqm";
let $params := map {
  "id": "abc123"
}
let $html := item:get-html($params)
(: Now we can verify the HTML returned by item:get-html ... :)
```

Improving code portability and sharing

As mentioned above, running a web application written in XQuery requires implementation-specific extensions—not necessarily to the language itself, but to provide functions specific to the HTTP context, for such things as accessing URL parameters of GET requests and setting HTTP response headers. As a result, one's codebase can quickly become peppered with implementation-specific function calls, resulting in code that not only requires extensive refactoring to port a web application from one XQuery implementation to another, but also inhibits sharing code with others, thereby promoting fragmentation within the XQuery community (Retter, §1.2). There are, however, some techniques that help alleviate this problem.

Using available standardizations

One such technique is to utilize what standardizations are available for XQuery web application development. The EXQuery organization (exquery.org) has proposed several specifications for standardizing functionality across XQuery implementations. Some of these proposals are specific to XQuery web application development, and of these the most widely implemented is RESTXQ. Proposed by Adam Retter in 2012, RESTXQ utilizes XQuery 3.0 annotations to associate URLs with XQuery functions (Retter). In other words, RESTXQ standardizes URL rewriting, the process whereby a clean, user-friendly URL accessed by the user (or by a program accessing a web service such as a REST API) is translated into a different URL that is actually used by the web application behind the scenes. More accurately, RESTXQ doesn't standardize URL rewriting so much as obviate the need for it altogether; instead of rewriting URLs from user-friendly to code-friendly, RESTXQ maps URLs to XQuery functions.

For example, returning to the commonplace behavior described above whereby a web application performs a search, leading to search results, leading to an item-level page for each result, let's say that any given item-level page is indicated by a URL in the format `/id/abc123` where `abc123` is a unique identifier for a particular item. In an implementation that supports URL rewriting, such as eXist or MarkLogic (Retter, §3.1.2 and §3.2.2), we could take `/id/abc123` and translate it to `?id=abc123` before handing it off to the XQuery processor, so that `id` is available as an HTTP request parameter name.

```
(: MarkLogic example :)
let $url:= xdmp:get-request-url()
let $regex-id := "/id/(.+)/?"
return
  if (fn:matches($url, $regex-id)) then
    (: extract identifier :)
    let $id := fn:replace($url, fn:concat("^.*", $regex-id, ".*$"), "$1")
    (: replace "/id/whatever" with "/" (implying "/default.xqy") and append "id=whatever" as a URL parameter :)
    let $separator := if (fn:contains($url, "?")) then "&" else "?"
    let $start := fn:replace($url, $regex-id, "/")
    return fn:concat($start, $separator, "id=", $id)
  (: else if ... :)
  (: else if ... :)
  else $url
```

Such URL rewriting code tends to be idiosyncratic and cumbersome, "creating a spaghetti of if/else statements" (Retter, §3.2.2). With RESTXQ, by contrast, `/id/abc123` can be simply and directly associated with a function, like so:

```
(: BaseX example :)
declare
%rest:path("/id/{$id}")
function c:get-item-view($id as xs:string)
{
  (: the variable $id has the value "abc123" :)
  ...
};
```

The RESTXQ approach is concise and straightforward, and it locates the URL mapping code at the function declaration itself (not in a separate "rewrite engine" module), leading to code that is easier to read and maintain. RESTXQ is supported in BaseX, eXist, and MarkLogic (Walmsley, p. 430), making it effectively a de facto standard. As a result, the code is portable across multiple implementations and shareable among developers and projects.

The use of RESTXQ can easily be incorporated into an MVC approach to code organization by adding RESTXQ annotations to functions in the controller (since the controller receives input from the HTTP request and takes action accordingly). Fleshing out the preceding example a little more:

```
(: BaseX example :)
module namespace c = "http://balisage.net/ns/Bal2016murr0319/controller";
import module namespace item = "http://balisage.net/ns/Bal2016murr0319/views/item" at "views/item.xqm";

declare
%rest:path("/id/{$id}")
%output:method("html")
%output:version("5.0")
function c:get-item-view($id as xs:string)
```

```
as element(html)
{
  (: the variable $id has the value "abc123" :)
  (: call the item-level view :)
  item:get-html($id)
};
```

Isolating implementation-specific functions

The main barrier to code portability across implementations and code sharing across the XQuery web development community is the necessity of implementation-provided functions. One technique to alleviate this problem is to abstract and isolate such functions. This goal can be achieved by creating one or more library modules containing generically named functions that internally utilize the corresponding implementation-specific functions. Then, throughout the codebase, whenever implementation-provided functionality is needed, we simply call the applicable generic function instead of the implementation-specific one. This approach creates a layer of abstraction, separating and hiding implementation-dependent code from the rest of the codebase. For example, we could create an "implementation" module and set up a generically named function for converting HTTP request parameters to an XQuery map, as shown above in a previous code example. Such a module written for BaseX would look like this:

```
xquery version "3.1";
(: BaseX example -- this module's filename is implementation-basex.xqm :)
module namespace imp = "http://balisage.net/ns/Bal2016murr0319/implementation";
import module namespace request = "http://exquery.org/ns/request";

declare function imp:http-params()
as map(*)
{
  map:merge(
    for $name in request:parameter-names()
    let $value := request:parameter($name)
    return map:entry($name, $value)
  )
};
```

The same functionality written for MarkLogic would look like this:

```
xquery version "1.0-ml";
(: MarkLogic example -- this module's filename is implementation-ml.xqy :)
module namespace imp = "http://balisage.net/ns/Bal2016murr0319/implementation";

declare function imp:http-params()
as map:map
{
  let $map := map:map()
  let $empty :=
    for $name in xdmp:get-request-field-names()
    let $value := xdmp:get-request-field($name)
    return map:put($map, $name, $value)
  return $map
};
```

Elsewhere in the codebase, whenever a map of HTTP parameters is needed, we can import the module appropriate to our current implementation and call the generically named function, `imp:http-params()`, rather than calling the implementation-specific function directly:

```
(: BaseX example :)
module namespace c = "http://balisage.net/ns/Bal2016murr0319/controller";
import module namespace imp = "http://balisage.net/ns/Bal2016murr0319/implementation" at "implementation-basex.xqm";

(: somewhere in some function ... :)
let $params := imp:http-params()
```

To target MarkLogic, the controller code would be identical except that the filename would be `implementation-ml.xqy` for the module import. Each "implementation" module acts as a kind of API for the rest of the web application code, such that we can change the underlying implementation without changing the outward-facing interface of the API. With this technique, sharing XQuery code from this web application with an individual or project using a different XQuery implementation, or even porting the entire application to a different implementation, could potentially only require swapping out one "implementation" module for another. Such a module could, of course, be utilized across multiple applications, rendering more and more of one's code implementation-independent.

Conclusion

When you have XML content that needs to be presented on the web, developing web applications with XQuery has notable advantages over the traditional technology stack and its accompanying web development frameworks. The techniques for web application development with XQuery described here are straightforward to apply, but they can have powerful and wide-ranging effects on the resulting code, leaving it more organized, readable, maintainable, testable, portable, and shareable.

References

[Kaufmann] Kaufmann, M., & Kossmann, D. (2009). Developing an enterprise web application in XQuery. Retrieved July 5, 2016, from https://www.semanticscholar.org/paper/Developing-an-Enterprise-Web-Application-in-XQuery-Kaufmann-Kossmann/6ddcffdaa35a836d21a73acf6b254e6ebc2b94e7. doi:10.1007/978-3-642-02818-2_39

[Retter] Retter, A. (2012). RESTful XQuery: Standardised XQuery 3.0 annotations for REST. Retrieved July 5, 2016, from http://adamretter.org.uk/papers/restful-xquery_january-2012.pdf

[Seiferle] Seiferle, M. (2012). Implementing web applications using XQuery: XML from front to back. Retrieved July 5, 2016, from http://files.basex.org/publications /Seiferle%20[2012],%20Implementing%20Web%20Applications%20Using%20XQuery.pdf

[Walmsley] Walmsley, P. (2016). *XQuery: Search across a variety of XML data* (2nd ed.). Sebastopol: O'Reilly.

Gregory Murray

<gregory.murray@ptsem.edu>

Director of Academic Technology and Digital Scholarship Services

Princeton Theological Seminary

Greg Murray has worked in web development and XML processing for 16 years, mainly in academic libraries. He is currently a project manager (who still codes as much as possible) helping develop web applications built with XQuery and MarkLogic Server for search and display of digitized library materials.

Balisage Series on Markup Technologies